An Early Start to Ourselves and Evolution with Life Processes

Roy Richards

SIMON & SCHUSTER

First published in Great Britain in 1991 by
Simon & Schuster Ltd
Wolsey House, Wolsey Road
Hemel Hempstead HP2 4SS

Printed in Great Britain by
BPCC Hazell Books, Paulton and Aylesbury

British Library Cataloguing in Publication Data

Richards, Roy
   An early start to ourselves and evolution (with life
   processes).
   1. Animals
   I. Title
   591

   ISBN 0-7501-0126-1

Series editor: John Day
Editor: Jane Glendening

ARTWORK ACKNOWLEDGEMENTS

Key: u: upper; m:middle; l:lower; L:left column; C:centre
column; R:right column

Lucy Su: 4, 5(uL, lL, uC, mC), 6(R), 8, 9(uL, uR), 10(uR),
11(lL, C, R), 15(uR, lR), 16, 17(L, uR), 19, 20(R), 21(R),
22(uL, uR), 27(mL, lC, R), 30(R), 31, 32(uR), 33–41, 44(lL),
50(L), 58, 60, 61, 64(lR), 71(lR), 75, 76(L)

Jane Cope/Linda Rogers Associates: 5(uR, lR), 6(L), 7,
9(mL, lL, C, lR), 10(L, lR), 11(uL), 12–14, 15(L), 17(mR, lR), 18,
20(L), 21(L), 22(lL, lR), 23–26, 27(uL, lL, uC), 28, 29, 30(L),
32(L, lR), 42, 43, 44(L, uR), 45–49, 50(R), 51–54, 56, 57, 59, 62,
63, 64(uL), 65–70, 71(u, lL), 72–74, 76(C, R), 77

Mansell Collection: 55

Anna Hancock: cover artwork

What is this book about? In a nutshell it is about Attainment Targets 1, 2, 3 and 4, at Key Stages 1 and 2, of the Science National Curriculum; that is exploration of science; the variety of life; processes of life and genetics and evolution. Used in conjunction with 'An Early Start to Nature' it will give comprehensive coverage of these areas. (At the time of going to press, it looks as though AT 1 is now to be called Scientific Investigation and ATs 2, 3 and 4 are to be combined into one attainment target: Life and Living Processes.)

I have left it to teachers to decide how to incorporate the activities set out in the book into their programmes of work but I have striven to suggest activities that are child centred, cross-curricular and, above all, fit into the context of primary teaching as I know it.

Children are always interested in themselves. I have made use of this interest when looking at life processes. At the same time I have attempted to show how those processes cut across the variety of life around us. Why we are all alike and yet all different from one another is touched

upon in the theme of variation which gives us a lead into the variety of life around us and into how present day forms of life have evolved from those present in the past. Put baldly, as it is in the National Curriculum as 'genetics and evolution', it seems perhaps alien to primary practice but on closer examination it is obvious that it is a theme we should take up with young children. The question is how to do so in a practical way that will appeal to and have meaning for young children. I hope that the activities suggested will have that practical appeal and give insight.

As in other books in this series children are introduced to the processes of:

- *exploring their environment in order to gather experiences at first hand*
- *manipulating objects and materials*
- *observing things around them*
- *questioning and arguing about things*
- *testing things out and performing simple problem solving activities*
- *looking for patterns and relationships.*

Safety in schools

All the activities in this book are safe provided they are properly organised and supervised in accordance with the recommendations of the DES, the Health and Safety Executive, the Association for Science Education, and local authority regulations. Any teachers who are uncertain about safety in scientific and technical work should consult their LEA advisers. They should also read 'Be safe: some aspects of safety in science and technology in primary schools', published by the Association for Science Education.

Red triangles

Some activities in this book do require extra care and attention. They are marked with a <u>red triangle</u>. Under no circumstances should children be allowed to pursue them unsupervised, particularly during breaks.

Always pack away potentially dangerous apparatus and chemicals immediately the activity is over.

Roy Richards

How fast?

How quickly can you cover a distance? Try walking 50 metres. No cheating, heel and toe gait all the way.

How quickly can you run 50 metres?

Keep records.

Name	Time taken to cover 50 metres	
	walking	running

Who is the fastest? Is it the tallest, shortest or longest legged child?

Breathing rate

Your breathing rate (and pulse rate) increases when you run.

Investigate breathing.

Count your breathing rate while sitting. This is quite difficult to do. Try to behave as naturally as possible. Time the rate over one minute.

Now jump on the spot for two minutes. Time your breathing rate for one minute afterwards.

Keep a record.

Name	Breathing rate	
	sitting	after jumping for 2 minutes

How long is it before your breathing rate returns to normal?

Measure your chest expansion

Measure one another's chest size.

Do this when your chest is at rest and when it is fully expanded.

Name	Chest size at rest	Chest size expanded	Chest expansion
	cm	cm	cm

Who has the biggest expansion?

Is this person the tallest?

Is it the person whose breathing rate returned most quickly to normal after exercise?

What is your lung capacity?

Is the child whose chest expands the most the one whose lungs hold the most air?

Take a 5 litre plastic bottle. Calibrate it by adding water half a litre at a time and marking the water level.

Turn the bottle upside down and number the graduations.

Fill the bottle with water and invert it into a <u>large</u> sink filled to a depth of at least 10 centimetres.

Insert a long length of plastic tubing.

Take a deep breath and then breathe out down the tubing. Pinch the tube shut as soon as you've finished. The drop in water levels gives a measure of lung capacity (in addition, there is a residual volume which you cannot breathe out).

Name	Chest expansion	Air expelled
	cm	cm³

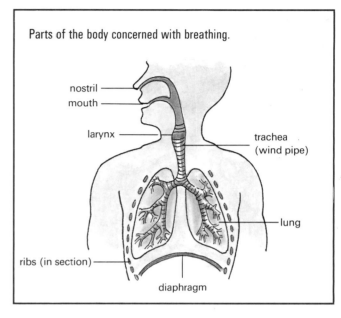

Parts of the body concerned with breathing.

nostril
mouth
larynx
trachea (wind pipe)
lung
ribs (in section)
diaphragm

Make a model of your lungs

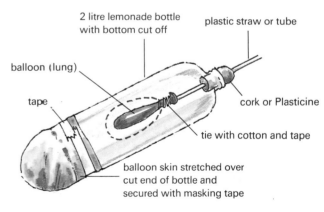

2 litre lemonade bottle with bottom cut off
plastic straw or tube
balloon (lung)
cork or Plasticine
tape
tie with cotton and tape
balloon skin stretched over cut end of bottle and secured with masking tape

Lowering the 'diaphragm' (a stretched balloon skin) shows how air is drawn into the lungs. It will cause the balloon to inflate slightly. The upward movement of the chest also helps to expand the lungs.

Such ventilation of the lungs is called <u>breathing</u>. It is <u>not</u> respiration. Respiration is the process by which energy is released from food.

Children are usually well aware of their heart beating and that there is a pulse at their wrist. The pulses at the neck and ankle are also fairly easy to find. These are all, of course, indications of the blood coursing through the body.

Find your pulse

Feel for your pulse in the hollow alongside the outermost bone near the wrist.

Press firmly but gently with two fingers. Do not use your thumb because it has a pulse of its own.

Changing pulse rates

Work in pairs.

One child lies down for two minutes. The other then takes this child's pulse for one minute, waits a further minute before taking the pulse again, and then waits another minute before taking the pulse for a third minute.

The child being tested now sits for two minutes before the pulse is again taken three times at one minute intervals.

The child now stands for two minutes. Then the tests are repeated as before.

Next the child runs on the spot for two minutes. Take the pulse at one minute intervals as before.

Keep records.

	Pulse beats in 1 minute			
	lying	sitting	standing	after running
1st reading				
2nd reading				
3rd reading				

Discuss when the pulse rate is lowest and when it is highest.

Discuss how the pulse rate increases when the blood has to carry more oxygen, which is used to help release more energy during exercise.

human circulatory system

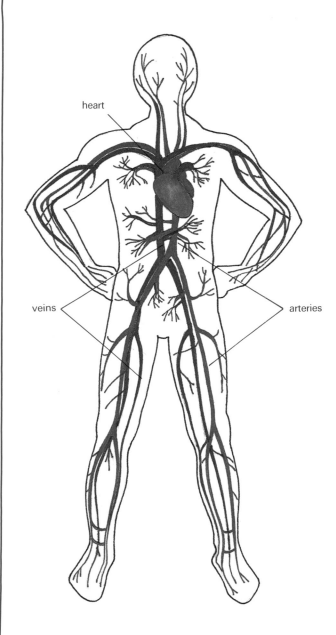

The circulatory system can seem inordinately complex to young children. Although it is interesting and informative for them to look at diagrams of the circulation like the one on the left, it is essential to show that it is really a very simple system.

The main point to emphasise is that it is a *double* circulatory system. Once from the heart and back via the lungs to pick up oxygen, then once round the body to deliver that oxygen before returning to the heart.

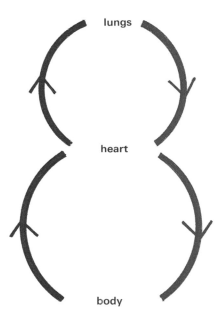

Bright red blood containing oxygen leaves the left ventricle of the heart and travels through the arteries to all parts of the body. The arteries eventually divide down into capillaries.

In the capillaries the blood gives up oxygen to the tissues. This is used to release energy from foods. This process is called respiration.

Carbon dioxide is produced as a waste product. The carbon dioxide is carried back through veins to the heart in dark red blood (*not* blue blood!).

The heart then pumps the blood, in the second part of the circulatory system, to the lungs. Here the carbon dioxide is given up and oxygen is absorbed. Bright red blood now flows from the lungs to the heart.

The vessels carrying blood away from the heart are called arteries. The vessels returning blood to the heart are called veins.

Blood

It is worth buying a blood slide from a scientific supplier in order to look at the structure of blood.

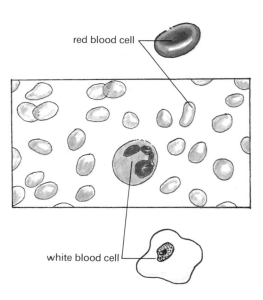

The red blood cells are easy to recognise by their disc shape. They contain a protein called haemoglobin which gives them their red colour. It is the haemoglobin which carries oxygen in the blood.

The white blood cells fight disease. They are irregular in shape and will have been stained so that they show up on the slide. There are few of these in comparison to the red blood cells.

Smell and taste are known as chemical senses because they respond to chemicals in food and in the environment. They are completely separate systems.

The nasal cavity at the top of the nose contains olfactory nerve endings which are sensitive to odorous particles in the air you breathe in. The tongue is covered by taste buds which respond to substances that dissolve in saliva. There are four basic components – sweet, salty, sour and bitter – that combine to give different tastes.

Warn the children of the dangers of smelling and tasting unknown substances.

Test your sense of smell

Collect a small range of everyday things with a distinctive smell. Test each other when blindfolded.

Name	Shoe polish	Banana	Cheese	Alm flav
Andrew	✓	✓	✗	

Test your sense of taste

Try taste tests while blindfolded.

Name	Apple	Orange juice	Onion	Hor
Carol	✓	✗	✓	

Relationship between smell and taste

Once children have tried a taste test they will realise that the texture of the food on the tongue often gives a strong clue to what they are tasting. It is important to remove this variable from tests. Chopping and mashing the food helps.

Collect a range of foods. Chop or mash them up. You could mash in bread as a neutral basis for each.

Do the test when blindfolded: first, firmly holding your nose closed, then with your nose open.

Wash your mouth out between each food tasting.

Food	Nose held	Nose open
apple	✗	✓

To discuss

Food often seems bland when we have a cold. This is because the nose is blocked and the smell of the food does not reach the receptors in the nose.

Test your smell fatigue

Hold a bottle of peppermint essence under your nose for at least three minutes.

Now try the range of things with a distinctive smell which you used in the smell tests on the opposite page.

Can you guess as many as before?

Can you tell margarine from butter?

For a stringent test, use several brands of butter, several brands of margarine and a fairly bland type of bread to try them on.

Randomise the order of presenting the butter and margarine samples for tasting.

Sugar or saccharine?

Can you tell sugar from saccharine?

You will probably need to try them in a familiar drink such as tea to make the test fair.

Dilution

Test the lowest concentration of a substance that can be tasted in a solution.

1 *Dissolve 10 grams of sugar in 100 cm³ of water in a tumbler.*

2 *Pour half of this into a second tumbler and make this up to the original volume (i.e. pour 50 cm³ of the first solution into the second beaker and add 50 cm³ of water). Stir.*

3 *Pour half of the second solution into a third beaker and make this up to the original volume. Stir.*

4 *Keep on diluting by equal volumes until you have ten solutions.*

Solution	Amount of sugar in 100 cm³
1	10·00g
2	5·00g
3	2·50g
4	1·25g
5	0·63g
6	0·31g
7	0·16g
8	0·08g
9	0·04g
10	0·02g

Starting with the weakest solution, taste each in turn until you can detect the sugar. Keep a record for each child in the class.

Repeat the test using salt instead of sugar.

Map your tongue

Test which areas of your tongue are sensitive to sweet (sugar solution), sour (lemon juice), salty (salty water) and bitter (strong coffee) tastes.

Use a medicine dropper to put tiny drops of each solution on different parts of the tongue.

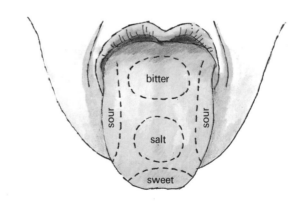

Some children find it difficult to distinguish different areas, but there is usually a consensus that the tip of the tongue is sensitive to sweet tastes. Sour receptors are at the sides, salt along the upper front part of the tongue and bitter tastes at the back of the tongue.

There are 20 deciduous or milk teeth in a young child. There are no premolars. An adult also has an extra pair of molars, in both the upper and lower jaws, called wisdom teeth.

milk teeth

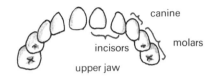

Adult teeth begin to appear at about 6 years. The second set of molars emerge at about 13 years and the third set (the wisdom teeth) any time in the next 15 years or so.

permanent teeth

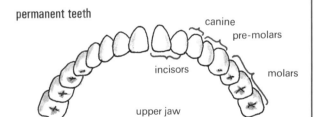

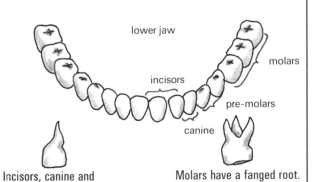

Incisors, canine and premolar teeth have one root.

Molars have a fanged root.

Use a mirror to help you make a drawing of your teeth.

Make a large clear drawing so you can see the shape of each tooth.

Model the teeth with coloured sticky paper.

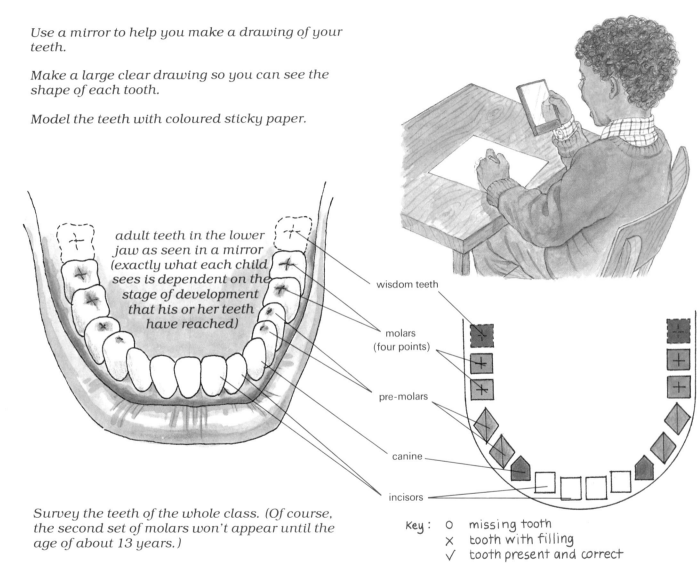

adult teeth in the lower jaw as seen in a mirror (exactly what each child sees is dependent on the stage of development that his or her teeth have reached)

wisdom teeth

molars (four points)

pre-molars

canine

incisors

Key:
- O missing tooth
- X tooth with filling
- ✓ tooth present and correct

Survey the teeth of the whole class. (Of course, the second set of molars won't appear until the age of about 13 years.)

Name	Lower right							Lower left						
	M	M	PM	PM	C	I	I	I	I	C	PM	PM	M	M

Make a graph of how often children clean their teeth.

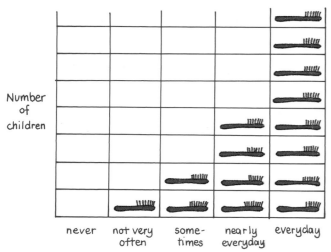

Number of children

never | not very often | some-times | nearly everyday | everyday

Cleaning teeth

Ask the children to bring a toothbrush.

Test 1

Eat a chocolate digestive biscuit. Clean your teeth.

Look at one another's teeth to see how well they have been cleaned.

Is brushing up and down better than brushing across?

Test 2

Again 'dirty' your teeth by eating a chocolate biscuit. Which method is best for cleaning them?

just rinsing

rinsing and brushing

eating an apple

electric toothbrush

Discuss why it is important to brush the gums as well as the teeth.

Plaster teeth

It is easy to make a plaster model of teeth.

Use fresh, unused Plasticine. Cut a slab about 15 millimetres thick and wide enough to just fit inside the mouth.

Put it onto a piece of thick card. Firmly bite into it once.

Plasticine

thick card

Take impressions of upper and lower jaws using separate blocks of Plasticine.

Grease each impression with olive oil.

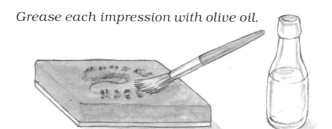

Mix some plaster of Paris – dental plaster is best. Once the plaster is smooth and creamy pour it onto your impression. Use a card surround to contain the plaster.

Leave the plaster overnight to set. Then remove the cast and clean it up with an old toothbrush.

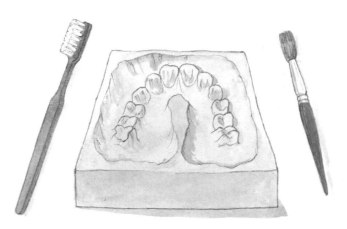

Paint the teeth in one colour and the background in another.

Carbohydrates, fats, proteins, mineral salts, vitamins and water are all needed for a healthy diet. Collect pictures from magazines and mount them to illustrate these food groups.

Carbohydrates

Fats

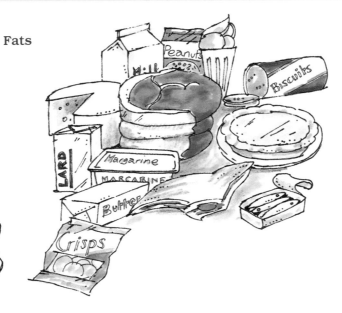

Mineral salts

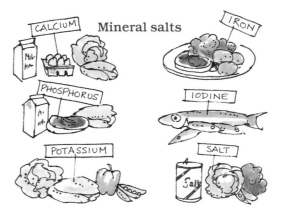

Proteins

Vitamins

Make a Venn diagram

Sort some of your pictures onto a Venn diagram.

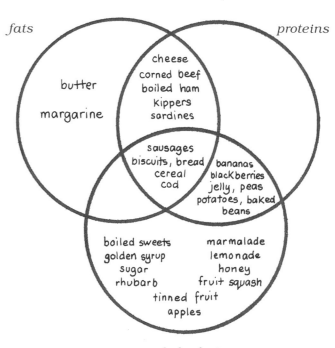

fats   *proteins*

butter
margarine

cheese
corned beef
boiled ham
kippers
sardines

sausages
biscuits, bread
cereal
cod

bananas
blackberries
jelly, peas
potatoes, baked
beans

boiled sweets
golden syrup
sugar
rhubarb
tinned fruit
apples

marmalade
lemonade
honey
fruit squash

carbohydrates

It is difficult, if not impossible, to find any foods which are pure protein or foods which are purely a mixture of fat and carbohydrate.

Food and energy

The foods we eat are broken down in the body and used both to build up new tissues and to produce energy.

From looking at labels on food, children will be familiar with some of the nutrients present in food and with some of the energy values they represent.

butter label

NUTRITION	TYPICAL VALUES PER 100g (3½oz)
ENERGY	3040k JOULES
	740k CALORIES
PROTEIN	0.5g
CARBOHYDRATE	less than 0.1g
TOTAL FAT	81.0g
of which POLYUNSATURATES	2.0g
SATURATES	49.0g
ADDED SALT	1.0g
VITAMINS	**% OF RECOMMENDED DAILY AMOUNT**
VITAMIN A	100%
VITAMIN D	30%

Energy is measured in joules. 1000 joules are 1 kilojoule (kJ). (The old unit, now superseded, was the calorie – 1 calorie is equivalent to just over 4 joules.)

1 joule is the amount of work done when a force of 1 newton moves an object a distance of 1 metre in the direction of the force. 1 newton (1 N) is the force required to produce an acceleration of 1 metre per second per second in a mass of 1 kilogram.

It requires a force of about 1 newton to support, say, an empty wine glass. You do about 1 joule of work if you lift the empty wine glass from the ground to a shelf 1 metre high.

Make a collection of food labels. Examine them to find the nutrients contained in the foods and to familiarise the children with the fact that energy values are marked in kilojoules.

Work out the energy value of a typical meal.

cereal label

NUTRITION INFORMATION per 100g	
ENERGY	1500kJ
	360kcal
PROTEIN	9.0g
CARBOHYDRATE	69.0g
of which sugars	26g
starch	43g
FAT	5.0g
of which saturates	3.0g
SODIUM	0.7g
FIBRE	7.0g
VITAMINS:	
NIACIN	16mg
VITAMIN B₆	1.8mg
RIBOFLAVIN (B₂)	1.5mg
THIAMIN (B₁)	1.0mg
FOLIC ACID	250µg
VITAMIN D	2.8µg
VITAMIN B₁₂	1.7µg
IRON	6.7mg

Peanut energy

It is important to show children the energy contained in food. The following demonstration is a powerful introduction.

1 Pour 10 cm³ of water into a boiling tube.
2 Put in a thermometer and record the temperature.
3 Ignite a peanut held on the end of a mounted pin by holding it in a candle flame.
4 As soon as the peanut begins to burn, hold it under the boiling tube to heat the water.
5 When the peanut stops burning, record the temperature of the water.
6 Repeat this several times using a fresh peanut and new water each time.

teacher demonstration

sheet of hardboard

Peanut	Temperature at start (°c)	Temperature at finish (°c)	Rise in temperature (°c)
1			
2			
3			
Average			

The rise in the temperature of the water is caused by the energy released from the peanut.

Making food

For baking bread and cakes and making butter, yoghurt and jelly, see 'An Early Start to Technology' (pages 88–89).

600kJ

210kJ

700kJ

1000 kJ

In the *mouth* food is broken down by chewing. There is some breakdown of starch to sugar.

Food is forced down to the stomach as the *gullet* alternately contracts and relaxes.

In the *stomach* milk clots. Proteins are broken down.

The *liver* produces bile, which helps break down fats.

The *pancreas* secretes digestive enzymes into the small intestine.

In the *small intestine* proteins, fats and carbohydrates are broken down, and the resultant products are absorbed.

In the *large intestine* there is some absorption of water. The waste material, mainly cellulose, is compacted for egestion.

The main stages in the breakdown of food are shown in the diagram. Although this process is unseen by children, they can be encouraged to read about it in suitable reference books.

The main points for discussion are:

1 proteins are broken down into building blocks (amino acids) that are used to build up the body tissues.

2 fats and carbohydrates are broken down (to glycerin and fatty acids, and glucose, respectively) to provide products rich in energy.

Fat can be stored under the skin and around the kidneys. Only limited amounts of carbohydrate can be stored, as glycogen in the liver and the muscles.

Excess protein cannot be stored. It is broken down into glucose and can be used to provide energy and a waste called urea which passes from the body in the urine.

Place the parts

Make a full-size body silhouette by drawing around someone.

Sketch the body parts by copying them from a book. Try to judge a suitable scale.

Pin the silhouette to the wall. Can the children judge the right places to pin the parts?

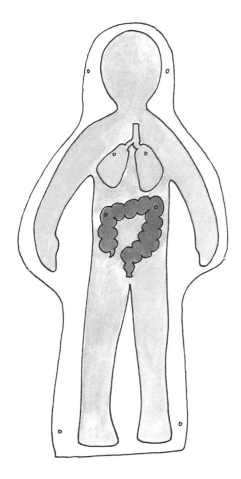

Much of the food taken in is used for growth. In children it is used to increase the body structure. Food provides energy for this process to occur.

Baby photographs

Collect baby photographs of the children in the class. Mount them on a wall. Put a number under each one.

Try to guess who each one is. Keep a record.

Photo number	Name
1	
2	

Discuss the results. Why are some easier to guess than others?

Discuss the changes that have occurred, such as growth of hair, increase in height, increase in girth, and bigger hands and feet. Note the relatively small increase in the size of the head.

A collection of outgrown clothes and shoes can make the basis for an interesting discussion.

Looking at growth patterns

Choose one child of average height from each class. Choose either all girls or all boys.

By observation and discussion draw out the differences that occur as children grow older. Look at height, waist size, hand size and so on. In general, are girls and boys about the same height?

Measuring growth patterns

Measuring human growth is a straightforward matter, but it is a long-term project.

In school more immediate results can be obtained by taking <u>one</u> child of average height for the class from each class in the school. Gather growth statistics about them.

Keep records.

Class	Height	Mass	Foot length	Foot width	Foot area	Hand span	Hand area
1							
2							

Is the growth pattern fairly constant from year to year, or are there sudden spurts?

Work uses energy. Energy is measured in joules.

> 1 joule of work is done when a force of 1 newton moves
> through a distance of 1 metre measured in the direction of the
> force.
>
> work = force × distance
> (joules)   (newtons)   (metres)

Children's understanding of energy and its units
is much improved by direct experience. For
instance, you do 10 joules of work if you move
10 newtons through one metre.

Make up some plastic carrier bags of sand. It
requires a force of approximately 10 newtons to
pick up 1 kilogram, so put 1 kilogram of sand into
each of the carrier bags. Tie them firmly around
the top.

You may need up to a dozen bags, depending on
the strength of the children.

Make a platform of large books on top of a table
so that the height of the top books is exactly
1 metre above the ground. You could cover the
books with a sheet of sugar paper or hardboard.

Lift the 1 kilogram bags one at a time onto the top
of the platform. Do this as fast as possible over a
period of 10 seconds.

Keep a record of the number of bags lifted.

Name	Number of sandbags lifted in 10 seconds

Calculate the work done

work = force × distance
(joules)   (newtons)   (metres)

For example, the work done in lifting one
10 newton sandbag 1 metre is

work = 10 newtons × 1 metre
       = 10 joules

If you lifted eight bags in the 10 seconds then

work = 8 × 10 newtons × 1 metre
       = 80 joules

Power

Power is the amount of work done in a certain
time. Power is measured in watts.

> 1 watt of power is produced when 1 joule of work is done in
> 1 second.

For example, if you did 80 joules of work in
10 seconds then

$$\text{work done in 1 second} = \frac{80}{10} \text{ joules}$$

so,

$$power = \frac{80}{10} \text{ watts}$$

$$= 8 \text{ watts}$$

Can you work out how many sandbags you
would have to lift to do the same amount of work
as that needed to keep a 60 watt bulb burning for
1 second?

Compare the work done in lifting the sandbags in
terms of joules with the energy values of the
foods on page 13.

Energy needed for 1 hour

walking on the flat
about 1200 kJ

running
about 2800 kJ

reading
about 400 kJ

painting
about 600 kJ

sleeping
about 350 kJ

Body temperature

Show how body temperature is taken. Disinfect the thermometer before use and leave it under your tongue for 2 or 3 minutes before taking a reading.

disinfectant

Show the children the constriction in the tube which causes a break in the mercury column when the thermometer is removed from the mouth, thus allowing a reading to be taken at leisure.

mercury

35

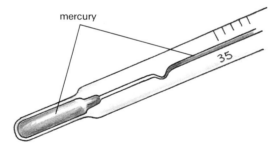

The themometer must be shaken before re-use to restore the complete column of mercury.

Normal body temperature is about 37°C.

Try taking your body temperature after taking a hot drink and after sucking an ice-cube.

Children can take their own body temperature using a forehead thermometer.

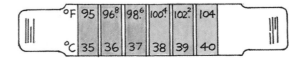

°F	95	96.8	98.6	100.4	102.2	104
°C	35	36	37	38	39	40

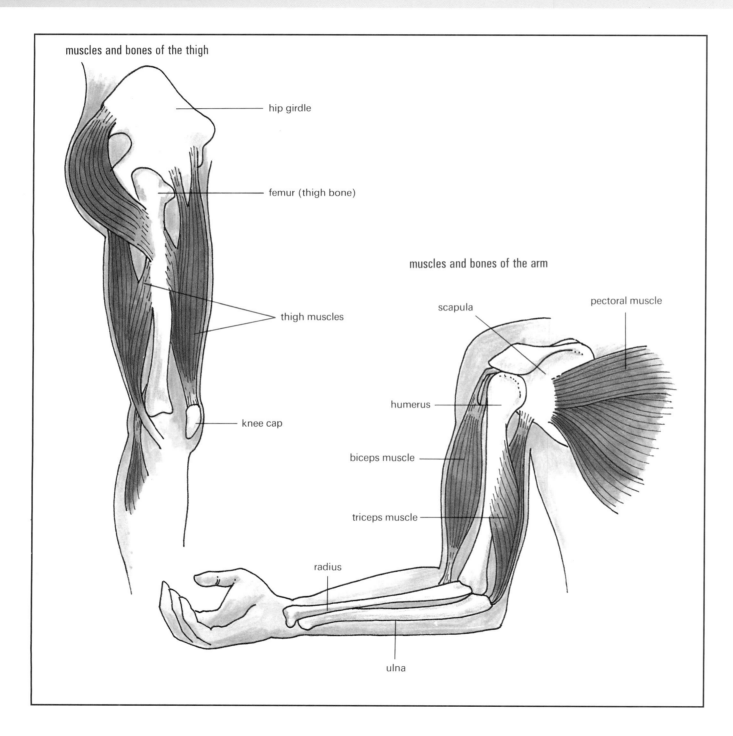

muscles and bones of the thigh

hip girdle

femur (thigh bone)

thigh muscles

knee cap

muscles and bones of the arm

scapula

pectoral muscle

humerus

biceps muscle

triceps muscle

radius

ulna

Make a model arm

This can be cut from thick card. Join the two limbs with a paper fastener.

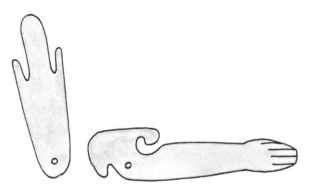

Use two short elastic bands: one to represent the triceps, and the other the biceps.

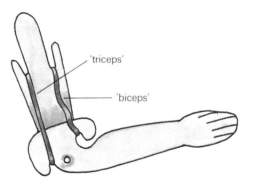

'triceps'

'biceps'

When the arm is straightened at the elbow it can be seen that the 'triceps' is short (contracted) and the 'biceps' long (relaxed).

Conversely, when the arm is bent at the elbow, the 'biceps' is short (contracted) and the 'triceps' long (relaxed).

See 'An Early Start to Technology' (pages 24–25) for more work on the skeleton.

How strong are your muscles?

You will need bathroom scales calibrated in newtons.

1 Push on the scales on the table. This uses your triceps. Can you feel them pulling?

2 Push on the scales with them between your hands. You are now using your pectoral muscles.

3 Put the scales under the table. Push upwards. This uses your biceps. Can you feel them pulling?

4 Push the scales against the wall with both legs. This uses your thigh muscles.

5 Test the strength of your fingers by squeezing the scales with your fingers.

Strong legs?

Pin a sheet of paper high on the wall. Reach up and make a mark on it (felt-pen ink on the fingertips works well).

Leap as high as you can and make a second mark.

Keep records.

Name	Reading in newtons for				
	triceps	biceps	pectorals	thighs	fingers

Analyse the results.

Which muscles produce most force?

Is there any correlation between the strength shown by different muscles and the height or mass of people?

The distance between the two marks shows your leaping power.

Keep a record.

Name	Distance leapt

Is there any correlation between leaping power and height, mass or thigh strength?

It is worth discussing the nature and the function of the skin. It is more than just a bag to hold us together. What interests children most are the parts that they can see.

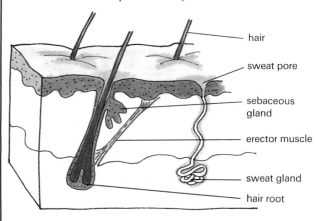

hair

sweat pore

sebaceous gland

erector muscle

sweat gland

hair root

Hairs are dead except right at the base. Oil produced by the sebaceous gland lubricates them. If the erector muscle attached to the hair contracts, we get goose flesh. The sweat glands produce sweat, which contains salt and a little urea.

Functions of the skin

1 It prevents entry of germs and protects us from mechanical injury.

2 It produces sweat and thus has an excretory function.

3 It is vital in regulating body temperature. Constriction and dilation of the blood vessels in the skin control the amount of blood present. When it is very hot, the vessels dilate, allowing more blood to the skin. Thus we go red. The blood heats up the sweat coming from the pores and causes it to evaporate. This process of evaporation removes heat from the body and cools us down.

4 It is waterproof.

5 It is sensitive to pressure, warmth, cold and pain (see page 23).

How much skin do we have?

Think of ways to work out how much skin each of us has. What is our total body surface area? Here are two suggestions.

Method 1

Using squared paper, cut cylinders of paper to fit the limbs. Make tubes for the main trunk of the body and so on so that you end up with a sort of paper suit of armour. Taper the cylinders so that they fit the limbs as exactly as possible.

Unwrap the cylinders and count squares to get a total body surface area figure.

For feet and hands draw outlines of the front and back of each.

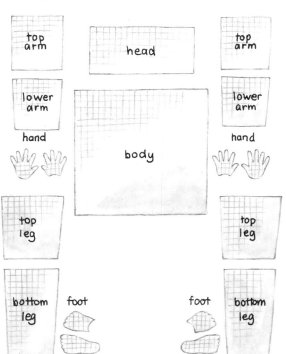

top arm

head

top arm

lower arm

lower arm

hand

body

hand

top leg

top leg

bottom leg

foot

foot

bottom leg

Method 2

Draw round a child stretched out on squared paper. If necessary join three or four sheets together.

Count all the squares covered. Include all those squares that are one-half or more covered, ignore squares that are less than half covered.

This only gives the area of the front (or back) of the body, so you need to double it to give a total back and front surface area. You still need to allow for the area of the sides of the body. You might judge these to be equivalent to one front (or back).

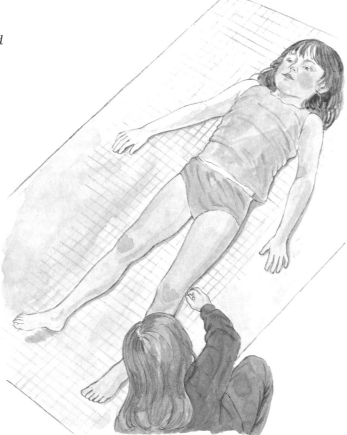

Skin patterns

Grooves form diamond-shaped patterns over much of the skin, but on the palms, fingers, soles and toes there are narrow parallel ridges and grooves. These make patterns of loops, whorls and arches.

Fingerprints

Experiment with different techniques of making fingerprints.

ink pad

wodge of blotting paper soaked with ink

print on black sugar paper with talc

There are four main fingerprint patterns.

loop   whorl   arch   composite

Collect prints from all the children. Hands vary, some carry only one type of pattern, whereas others have a number of patterns on the one hand.

No two people, not even identical twins, have the same pattern.

Forensic science

The use of fingerprints in detective work was pioneered in the 19th century, notably by Francis Galton (1822–1911). In the UK, Sir Edward Henry, commissioner of the Metropolitan Police from 1903 to 1919, helped develop the technique for police work.

Detective work

Take the fingerprints of ten children.

In addition, in secret, take a second set of prints from one of the ten. Swear this child to secrecy.

Can the others work out whose prints they are?

Boys and girls

It has been reported that women have a higher degree of sensitivity in their fingertips than men because their finger ridges are less prominent. Is this true for girls and boys? Make a survey. Then try some tests (see page 22).

Try a 'feely' test. Make a small collection of common classroom objects to hide in a bag. Can others identify them by touch alone?

Name	Paperclip	Rubber	Pencil	Chalk	Key	

Make various collections to test people.

collection of shapes

collection of coins

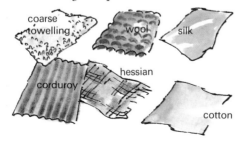

collection of fabrics

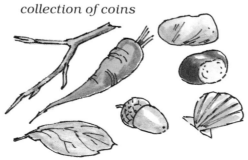

collection of natural things

Try feeling with your toes

Are they as sensitive as your fingertips?

Use an empty washing up bowl to prevent objects getting away.

Object	Name:		Name:		Name:
	Fingers	Toes	Fingers	Toes	Fingers

More difficult touch tests

Sort different grades of sandpaper. This is usually available in packs of four grades from DIY shops. Mix two sets and sort from the coarsest to the finest by touch alone.

Sort papers and card by thickness.

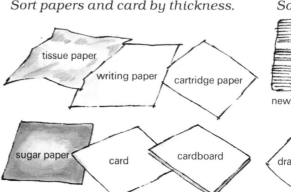

Sort papers by texture.

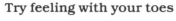

Nervous system

Stimulation of the touch receptors causes an impulse to pass along peripheral nerves into the spinal cord and hence to the brain. Thus we feel the sensation of touch (or pressure).

There are also receptors in the skin which are sensitive to warmth, cold and pain.

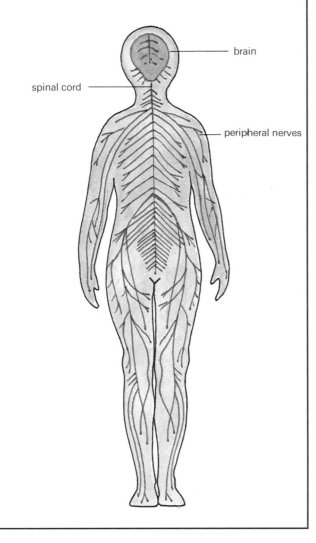

brain

spinal cord

peripheral nerves

Compare the sense of touch of different parts of the body.

Use a hairpin with the points set 2 centimetres apart.

2cm

Blindfold a child. Let a partner try touching the child gently with the points of the hairpin. Use a mixed pattern of touching: sometimes using one point and sometimes two.

Touch all over the body: fingertips, palm, arm, neck, cheek, chin, forehead, back, chest, thigh, leg, sole of the foot and toes.

Each time the child must say whether one or two points are felt. Be careful!

Keep a record. Use a ✓ for each correct response and a X for each incorrect one.

Name:	Fingertips	Palm
Katie	✓ ✓ ✓ ✓ ✓ ✓ ✓ ✓ ✓ ✓	
Arm	Neck	Cheek
Chin	Forehead	Back
		X X X X X ✓ X X X X
Chest	Thigh	Calf
Foot top	Foot sole	Toes

Draw round a child to make a body outline. Use different colours or shading to show the sensitivity of different body parts.

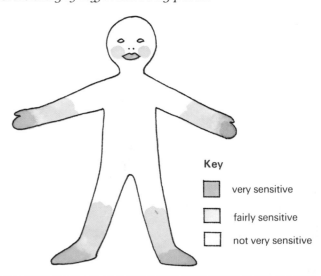

Key

▦	very sensitive
▢	fairly sensitive
☐	not very sensitive

A person drawn in proportion to the relative sensitivity to touch of different regions of the body.

The hands, lips and soles of the feet are the most sensitive parts.

cross-section of human eye

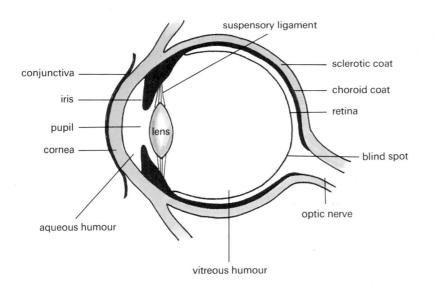

The eye is a hollow ball-shaped object with the wall of the ball made of three layers.

The *sclerotic coat* is a white opaque outer layer with a transparent part at the front called the *cornea*. The cornea is covered by a thin transparent protective layer called the *conjunctiva*.

The *choroid coat* is a thin middle layer which is black. It is thicker at the front of the eye, where it forms a muscular body to which the *suspensory ligaments* are attached. These support and control the shape of the lens. The *iris* or coloured part of the eye is also part of this layer.

The *retina* is the innermost layer of the eye. It contains light-sensitive cells called *rods* and *cones*.

The *lens* separates the two parts of the eye. The very small front part is filled with a watery fluid called *aqueous humour*. The large rear part is filled with a jelly-like material called *vitreous humour*.

Ask the children to work in pairs. Each makes a careful drawing of one of the other's eyes.

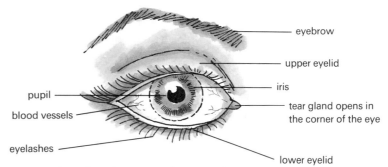

How many eyes of each colour are there in the class? Make a chart.

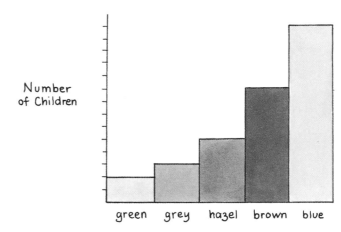

Blind spot

Close your left eye. Look at the cross shown above while holding the book about 50 centimetres from your face. Move the book gradually towards your face. Does the black spot disappear?

When it disappears, light from the black spot is falling onto the blind spot of your eye. This is where the optic nerve leaves the eye. There are no light-sensitive cells in this area.

Light rays travel in straight lines. They can be bent (refracted) by a lens.

The lens in the eye is elastic and changes shape to focus light rays onto the light-sensitive cells in the retina. This change of shape is caused by contraction and relaxation of the ciliary muscles which in turn pull on the suspensory ligaments, which are attached to the lens.

Looking at distant objects

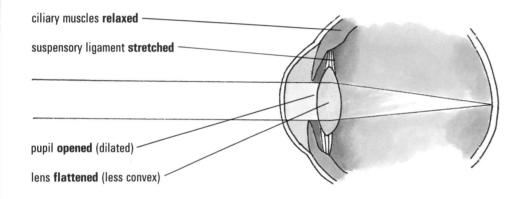

ciliary muscles **relaxed**

suspensory ligament **stretched**

pupil **opened** (dilated)

lens **flattened** (less convex)

Looking at near objects

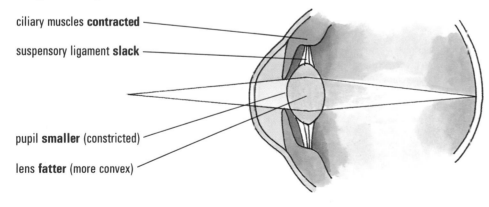

ciliary muscles **contracted**

suspensory ligament **slack**

pupil **smaller** (constricted)

lens **fatter** (more convex)

Long sight

To look at near objects we contract the ciliary muscles and increase the converging power of the lens so that the light rays are focused on the retina.

In some people the eye cannot adjust (accommodate) for this and the light rays are focused behind the retina. This can be corrected by wearing spectacles with convex lenses.

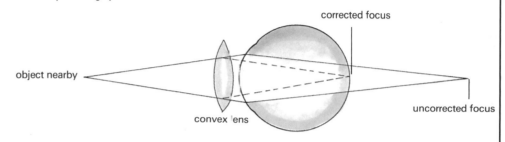

corrected focus

object nearby

convex lens

uncorrected focus

Infants are long sighted because they have an adult size lens before the eye is fully grown. Light from near objects is focused behind the retina. This effect disappears as they grow.

Short sight

Short-sighted people have difficulty focusing on distant objects. This usually happens because the eyeball has become too long, and so the light rays focus in front of the retina.

Concave lenses, which cause light rays to diverge, are used to correct this condition.

uncorrected focus

corrected focus

light rays from distant object

concave lens

Upside down

The image received at the back of the eye is upside down. The brain 'corrects' this and we see things the right way round.

Light rays travel in straight lines. Rays from the top of the match head are brought through the lens to a point on the retina where they are directly below those brought from the bottom of the match.

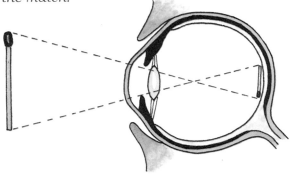

Make a pin-hole camera

The inversion of images is easily shown with a pin-hole camera.

Use a cylindrical cardboard container, such as those used to hold talcum powder. (Alternatively, you could use a tin with a press-on lid and amend the construction.)

1 Make a tiny pin-prick hole in the bottom of the container.

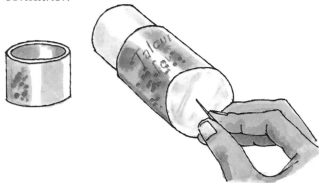

2 Cut out the main central part of the lid with scissors.

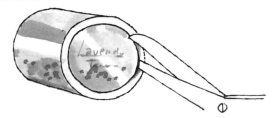

3 Put greaseproof paper over the end of the container. Press on the lid.

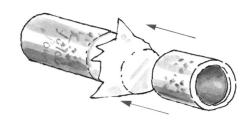

4 Make a black-paper sleeve to fit over the container.

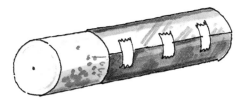

5 Hold the camera towards a bright light source such as a burning candle. You will see an upside down image of the candle on the greaseproof paper.

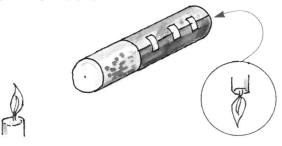

Persistence of vision

The eye can retain successive images. This is easily demonstrated by making a simple Victorian toy called a thaumatrope.

Cut a card disc about 7 centimetres in diameter.

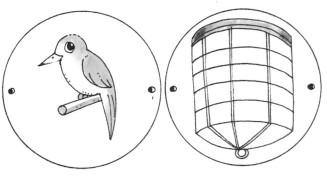

Draw a bird on one side and a cage on the other. Draw the cage upside down.

Pierce a hole either side of the disc. Thread with thin strings. Twirl the disc to see the bird in the cage.

Alternatively, you could draw on either side of the card with both figures upright. Insert the card in a split-cane and revolve it between your hands.

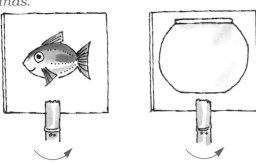

Too much light

Work in pairs. Let one child make a careful drawing of one of his or her partner's eyes. Stress that it is especially important to record the size of the pupil. Do this in normal classroom light.

Now let the child whose eye has been drawn sit either in a dimly lit room or with a cardboard box over his or her head for 5 minutes.

viewing slit

Re-draw the eye.

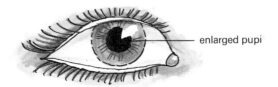

enlarged pupil

The eye adjusts to let in more light. The pupil is a mechanism for controlling the amount of light entering the eye. We squint in a sudden bright light to quickly reduce the amount of light entering the eye.

If you make a pupil-size scale you can record the actual change in size of the pupil under different lighting conditions.

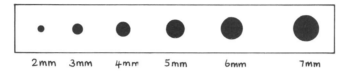

2mm   3mm   4mm   5mm   6mm   7mm

Blinking

Blinking is a mechanism for lubricating and protecting the eye.

We have some control over blinking. Some people can stop blinking for long periods. Children are very fond of playing a game where they stare one another out.

An interesting demonstration of blinking as an involuntary protective mechanism is to stand a child on one side of a window and then throw a crumpled paper ball at the child's face. Invariably, the child blinks.

Try these tests.

Stare someone out. How long is it before one of you blinks? Keep a record. Who is the class champion.

Find out if people blink more under certain conditions. For example, test each other when
    doing mathematics
    painting
    reading a book
    talking.

It might affect your blinking rate if you know you are being tested so devise ways of doing it without the 'victim's' knowledge.

Tell someone you are going to read a passage from a book to them. Let them think that you are going to test them on what is read. While you are reading, someone else can count how many times the listener blinks, say over one minute.

This is one way of standardising the test for a number of people.

What conclusions about rate of blinking can you make from these tests?

Sometimes images trick our brain. The world of optical illusions is an intriguing one for children.

Just lines

Which horizontal line is longer, A or B?

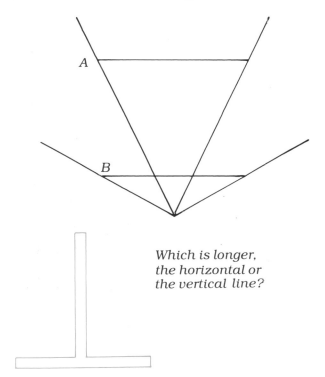

Which is longer, the horizontal or the vertical line?

Are all these lines straight?

Which vertical line is the longest?

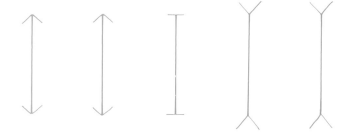

Which horizontal line is longer?

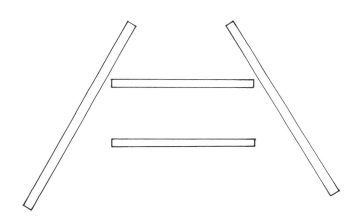

Are the red lines curved? Check with a ruler.

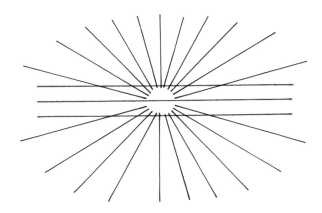

Could you make these 3D objects?

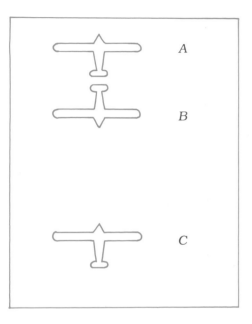

Is the nose of aircraft A or aircraft C nearer to the nose of aircraft B?

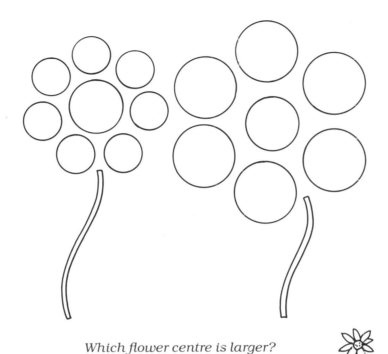

Which flower centre is larger?

Is it a vase or two faces?

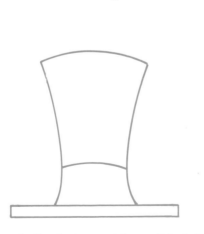

Is the hat as wide as it is tall?

Which of these two vases is wider at the top and bottom?

Is it a rabbit or duck?

Can you see grey spots where the white lines cross?

Can you see a young woman *and* an old woman?

You can use a conventional optician's chart, with children who can identify letters accurately.

Z
DE
FHP
NVRU
ZDEFH
PENRUZ
VZDHPERU
DHVERPUP

Alternatively, you can use an eye chart like the one on the right.

To use the E-chart, cut out a large E using the template below.

The children can test each other in turn. The child under test has to move the cut-out E to the same position as the one indicated by the child conducting the test.

A child with normal vision will be able to read right to the bottom line.

Have someone keep a record of where each child gets to.

3m

Increasing the distance makes the test more difficult and makes it possible to put the children into order of seeing ability.

Test right eyes alone. Test left eyes alone.

Test a group of children who all wear glasses. Test them with and without their glasses.

Are there any correlations with the details of long and short sight on page 25?

Hold the bottom end of a pen in front of you, but not at arm's length. With both eyes open, lower the top onto it. Try this again but with your left eye, and then your right eye, closed.

Is it easier with one eye closed?

Try to touch the tip of a pencil held out by another child with the tip of your own pencil.

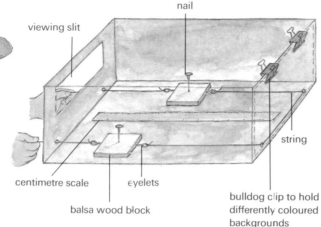

Now try this with your right eye closed, and then with your left eye closed.

Both these simple tests show that two eyes are better than one for judging distance.

Here are two more tests to try.

Put two identical toy cars in line with one another. Tie a piece of string to a third car.

Pull the string until it lines up the third car with the other two. Now try doing this with each eye closed in turn.

Make the testing box shown below from a shoe box.

viewing slit

nail

string

bulldog clip to hold differently coloured backgrounds

centimetre scale

eyelets

balsa wood block

How easy is it to line up the nails? Do it with both eyes open. Then try with each eye closed in turn.

Try with different coloured backgrounds too. Do some colours help?

Peripheral vision

We have evolved as hunting animals and our senses are directed forward. We use our sense of sight especially for stimuli from the front. Consequently, our peripheral vision, if compared with animals like birds or fish, is quite restricted.

The following method is a fairly straightforward way of measuring peripheral vision.

Tie a piece of string across the centre of a PE hoop. Mark the centre of the string. Rest the hoop on the backs of two chairs, as shown.

Seat a child in the centre with the string touching the bridge of his or her nose. By this means you can centre each child quickly.

Ask the seated child to stare straight ahead at a mark on the wall.

Slowly move a pencil around the edge of the hoop starting from behind the child's head. When the child sees the pencil, mark the hoop with chalk. Do this on both sides of the head. This gives an indication of each person's peripheral vision.

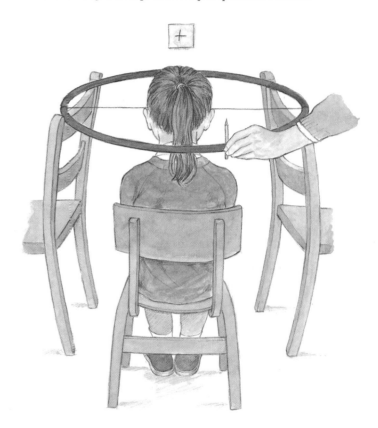

Try it with differently coloured pencils, red, blue, green etc. How soon can each person tell the colour of the pencil?

Road safety

A good depth of vision and peripheral vision are both very important in our daily lives. The ability to judge distance and the need for good peripheral vision when driving a car or crossing the road are useful discussion topics.

Hearing

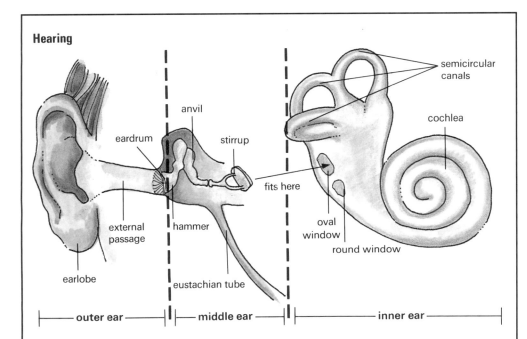

semicircular canals

anvil

cochlea

eardrum

stirrup

fits here

external passage

hammer

oval window

round window

earlobe

eustachian tube

outer ear — middle ear — inner ear

Sound waves pass down the external passage of the ear and cause the eardrum to vibrate. These vibrations pass through three small bones in the middle ear: the hammer, the anvil and the stirrup. The stirrup is attached to the oval window, an opening into the inner ear which is covered by a delicate membrane.

Vibrations pass from this membrane to a fluid inside a bony structure called the cochlea. Vibrations of this fluid cause impulses to pass along the auditory nerve to the brain and we hear the sound.

The middle ear is connected to the back of the throat by a narrow tube called the eustachian tube. This tube is open to the mouth when we swallow. It allows air to pass through to equalise the pressure on either side of the eardrum.

Balance

The semicircular canals contain a fluid which moves as we move. This fluid controls our sense of balance. If we spin round and round it goes on spinning for a short time after we stop and gives us a feeling of giddiness.

Balance

The ear is an important organ of balance.

Examine how it can help us to balance, and thus help us to find direction (to some extent) if we are blindfolded.

Get a child to walk as straight a line as possible. Mark his or her route with a chalk line.

Now blindfold the child. Try again.

Try other children.

How good are they at judging a straight line?

How many children go to the right?

How many children go to the left?

Water sounds

Guessing the nature of containers by the sound made by water squirting into them can be fun.

Set up some plastic syringes as shown by sticking the nozzles through holes in card.

Can you guess whether the water is hitting glass, plastic or tin?

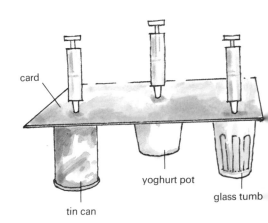

card

yoghurt pot

glass tumbler

tin can

Indoors/outdoors

Tape record various sounds. For example,
<u>*indoors*</u>*: voices, plumbing, chair scraping, breathing, clock ticking, toilet flushing, telephone ringing, radio, footsteps*
<u>*outside*</u>*: birds, traffic, sirens, train, rain, aeroplane, pelican crossing, thunder, footsteps.*

Can the children identify the sounds when you play them back to the class?

Can they put words to the sounds? For example, 'crunch' for footsteps on gravel and 'swish' for cars passing.

Matching 'concertos'

Play a note to a friend. Can your friend match it?

Try matching two notes, three notes and so on.

Who can match most notes in a sequence?

Tumbling tins

Collect some tins. The sort of cocoa tin with a press-on lid is useful.

Put a different object in each – a wooden cube, a piece of cotton wool, seeds, a paper clip, a coin, a feather, some treacle, air, a pencil stub, a rubber, a biro top and so on.

Shake the tins. Can you guess what is inside from the sound?

Keep a record.

Name	Coin	Cottonwool	Se
Joe	✓	✗	
Rajah	✗	✗	

Tapping tunes

Tap an empty bottle with a pencil. Listen to the sound.

Slowly fill the bottle with water, but keep tapping as you do so.

What happens to the sound?

Collect seven empty bottles. Pour water into each to different levels.

Tap the bottles. Listen to the note. The water and the bottle are vibrating.

Blow over the tops. Listen to the note. The air in the bottle is vibrating.

How well can you hear?

It is surprising how well sound travels.

You will need a quiet, constant sound source for this test. A clock with a soft tick is suitable.

Set the clock a good distance away from you, for example, across the school hall.

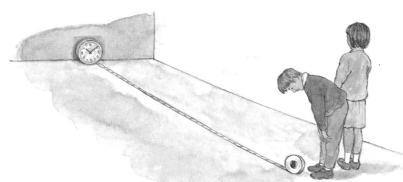

Advance slowly towards the clock. Stop when you can hear the tick.

Measure your distance from the clock.

Name	Distance from clock

By this means you can sort people in order of hearing ability.

Now muffle the sound of the clock by smothering it with newspaper in a box. Try the test again to find out how near you can get before you hear the clock.

This will of course take you into the realm of sound insulation. Try a range of insulators.

Name	Distance from clock surrounded by :		
	newspaper	cotton wool	polystyrene bits

Sound travelling

Sound travels through solids, liquids and gases. We normally hear sounds coming through the air.

Try to enhance their volume by making an ear trumpet.

card or sugar paper

sticky tape

large enough opening to fit over the ear

Fit a piece of dowel rod into the end of a plastic funnel. This makes a listening device rather like that used by officials from the water board.

Place it against a ticking seconds timer. You will hear the sound travelling up the wooden rod – that is, travelling through a solid.

ticking watch

Alternatively, listen to a ticking watch by placing your ear on a table top.

Sounds through liquid are more difficult to experience. If you take a hammer and a piece of metal pipe to the swimming baths, you can strike the pipe in water by kneeling at the deep end.

Those children unafraid to put their head under water can do so at the shallow end and listen. It is a wonderful sound rather like a church bell tolling.

Our evolution as hunting animals has led to sight being the dominant sense in detecting stimuli in front of us. Although hearing is used for sounds coming at us, it is used even more for sounds from the sides and from behind.

Sit a child centrally in the school hall. Blindfold the child. Distribute the rest of the class randomly around the hall. Give each child a pair of coins.

Ask the children, one at a time, but keeping a random order, to tap one coin against another.

The blindfolded child has to point to where the sound comes from.

Keep a record. A system of ticks and crosses will do.

Name	In front	Left side	Right side	Behind

The test can be made more stringent by making sounds not only at waist height but also near the ground and above the head.

Name	In front			Left side			Right side			Behind		
	high	middle	low	high	middle	low	high	middle	low	high	middle	low

Sounds from the sides are usually located with ease, but sounds from the front, rear and above are more difficult to locate.

The senses of sight and hearing are complementary: sight for frontal stimuli and hearing for sounds from the side.

It is interesting to try the test with one ear stopped up. This completely throws your sense of sound direction.

Pitch

Different objects make different sounds: some high, some low.

Make a collection of objects that will make a sound.

Sit the class in a circle on the floor, each with a sound-making object.

Each child in turn makes a sound with an object, with everyone else paying careful attention. Talk about each sound, about its loudness and its pitch.

Turn the circle to face outward. Each child, in turn, again makes a sound with an object but, of course, the rest of the class can't see. Can the children guess the object by the sound alone?

Does familiarity with the objects help? Are high sounds easier to recognise than low sounds?

It is a commonly held belief that we have five senses, but the body is more complex than this.

For example, we have a sense that makes us aware of where our limbs are and of what we have to do to move various parts of our body. This is called the kinaesthetic sense.

The receptors for it are present in our muscles, tendons and ligaments. These receptors act, together with the receptors of the semicircular canals in our inner ear, to give us a sense of balance.

Here are some tests to illustrate this sense.

Hands apart

Ask a blindfolded child to touch either side of an object.

Remove the object. Ask the child to put his or her hands together and then move them apart to the same width as the object.

Keep records.

Name	Object	Actual length	Estimated length	Error
	book			
	tray			
	metre rule			
	book			
	tray			

How heavy?

Work in pairs. Blindfold one partner and place a yoghurt pot containing a little water on the palm of his or her hand.

The other partner slowly and quietly adds water a few drops at a time to the yoghurt pot.

The blindfolded child indicates when a change in the weight of water in the yoghurt pot is felt.

Keep a record.

Name	Test 1	Test 2	Test 3	Average

What is the smallest volume of added water detected? It is surprising how accurate children become at these tests with a little practice.

Gather together four identical boxes. Flat chocolate boxes are ideal, as are the boxes that hold half-a-dozen mince pies or apple tartlets. Partition the boxes as shown using card or small boxes secured with glue or tape.

Put a marble in each box. Close the lids. If you stick them down, number the boxes and keep a note what partitioning is inside each.

By using their kinaesthetic sense and by listening, children can attempt to construct a mental image of what is in the box by gently moving the box in their hands. The movement of the marble will give lots of clues.

Try the same experiment with wooden boxes; cigar boxes are ideal. Use balsa wood for the partitions. You can make up all sorts of partitioning.

One of the characteristics of living things is their ability to respond to their environment. At a simple level the stimulus–response mechanism can be studied by measuring the time between the stimulus and the response. This is called the reaction time.

Here are some suggestions for tests that children can carry out on one another.

Catch a marked card or ruler

Hold up a ruler. Ask a partner to flank the base of the ruler with forefinger and thumb (not touching the ruler).

Drop the ruler. How quickly can your partner catch it?

The distance up the ruler is a measure of the time taken to catch it.

Keep a record.

Name	Tries		Average
	1		
	2		
	3		
	1		
	2		

Some variables to check are that:

(a) every test starts with finger and thumb flanking the base of the ruler
(b) the time interval between drops is varied so that the person under test cannot guess when the ruler is about to be dropped
(c) the distance apart of finger and thumb is fairly constant for each test.

You could use a strip of card marked at 2 centimetre intervals for younger or less able children to try. Number the intervals, so the children can record their scores.

The template on the left is marked in fractions of a second. The distances have been worked out by calculating how fast the ruler falls under the pull of gravity.

Copy the template onto a suitable piece of card to give you a reaction timer, where the time can be read directly from the scale.

0·27	0·26	0·25	0·24	0·23	0·22	0·21	0·20

0·19	0·18	0·17	0·16	0·15	0·14	0·13	0·12	0·11	0·10	0·09	0·08	0·07	0·06	0·05

Avoiding a dropped pebble

Drop a pebble from a fixed mark on the ruler, at say 25 cm.

Can your partner avoid the pebble? If he or she succeeds, try dropping it from a lower mark.

Keep a record.

Name	Lowest mark from which pebble misses hand

Test foot reaction times too. Don't use a large pebble!

More experiments

Measure reaction times:
  first thing in the morning
  before lunch
  after lunch
  at the end of the day.

Are girls faster than boys?

Test the school staff. Age is a factor!

Group reaction times

Stand facing outwards in a circle and hold hands.

Appoint a leader to hold a stopwatch in one hand. The person standing on this side of the leader holds the leader's wrist.

The leader starts the stopwatch and simultaneously squeezes the hand of the person holding his or her free hand. This person in turn squeezes the hand of the person alongside and so on.

When the squeeze has passed right round the circle, the last person (the one holding the leader's wrist) squeezes the leader and the leader stops the stopwatch.

We thus have an idea of the group's reaction time.

Variables which will arise from discussion with the children are:
(a) they can see the squeeze as it goes around (some children will probably suggest doing the test with eyes closed)
(b) they can hear the click of the stopwatch as it starts (some children will suggest muffling the stopwatch, some will suggest putting cotton wool in ears).

Children often want to vary this test, for instance by:
  sending the squeeze the other way
  facing inwards in the circle.

Memory varies between people. A good memory is a precious asset.

Here are some tests to measure how well people remember things.

Kim's game

This is a popular party game with young children. It is named after Kim, the hero in one of Rudyard Kipling's stories. Kim was trained as a spy.

Put ten objects on a tray. Let the children look at them for one minute. Then cover them.

How many objects can each child remember?

Keep a record.

Name	Number remembered		
	1st try	2nd try	3rd try

Do children get better with practice?

Increase the number of objects to fifteen by adding five new objects. What happens?

Choose fifteen new objects. What difference does this make?

Discuss the strategies used for memorising. Many children remember by picturing the objects in place. Some link some of the objects in various ways.

Does colour help memory?

Make up 3 × 3 grids on card. Make them with different background colours. Use white, red, blue, black, yellow and so on.

Collect some plain coloured toy cars all of the same type. Vary the colour, say two white, two red, two green, one yellow, one black and one orange.

Test your ability to remember their colours when placed on different coloured backgrounds.

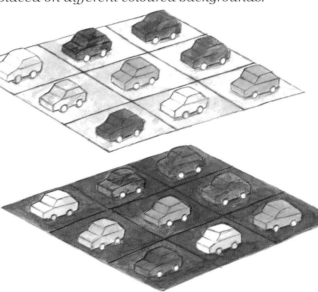

Does the background colour affect memory?

Vary the arrangements of the cars.

Vary the number of cars of any one colour in each test.

Increase the size of the grid if the test becomes too easy.

Can you come to any conclusions about colour and memory?

3 *Now try the test using words.*

Words
elephant, chair, spoon
brick, dog, wood, onion
house, tree, mushroom, leg, table
water, girl, book, road, toffee, fire
fibre, jam, thermometer, nail, button, skeleton, grass

4 *Test each child's memory for sentences.*

Choose sentences from a book or make some up. You need say four sentences of about ten, fifteen, twenty and twenty-five words. Read each out in turn to find out how well the children remember them.

You will find that meaning helps a lot with memorising. Make up a nonsense sentence and try that out too.

Analysis

In each of the tests the number of items remembered constitute the 'memory span'. Children usually score best on the figures with their memory span for letters and isolated words being lower.

Particular sounds are more memorable. The fading of the 'ee' sound is particularly prone to retention. For example, 'three' or letters like B, C, D, E, G, P, T and V.

Keep a record for this and subsequent tests.

Name	How many remembered			
	figures	letters	random words	sentences

1 Ask a child to read aloud the figures in the table below to each child in the class in turn.

Figures
3 2 1   9 5 4
7 2 6 3 2 1   5
8 9 2 4 7 3 9 1
2 7 6 3 4 9 8 1   7
5 3 2 4   1 5 9 7 1   8

Read one line at a time. Say the figures evenly – one per second. The child being tested must try to repeat each line of figures once they have been read out.

How many figures can each child remember?

2 Repeat the test but using letters.

Letters
J   C   Q   B
L   M   B   Z   S
G   K   N   M   T   H
K   S   X   F   H   L   P
O   C   E   P   Q   M   B   E
Z   B   F   S   O   D   F   G   M

Any study of ourselves would be incomplete without consideration of our life cycle. It is the same as that of other mammals, with a pattern of egg production, development to maturity, mating and egg production. However, reproduction is inevitably tied up with sex education and the whole process is overlaid with social factors.

The way it is dealt with will vary considerably with the differing views of teachers, parents and governors. There is a wide range of moral, ethical and social issues surrounding the topic, all of which demand attention.

There is no attempt here to describe the reproductive organs and the act of coition. The details are to be found in many books, and whether they are used, and the sensitivity with which this particular aspect of the topic is dealt with, can only be left to individual teachers and to the policy of individual schools.

What is attempted here is a broad outline that may have appeal to a wide range of teachers and schools.

Cells

The idea of cells is difficult for young children. Usually they will not have had the experience of looking at sections of tissues and preparations of cells on slides that is part of secondary-school work. However, cells are part of the vocabulary of modern life.

A cork from a wine bottle often shows the cellular structure of which it is made.

Cells are the basis of life. The sperm from a man joins with the egg from a woman. This is called fertilization.

The sperm and the egg are tiny. They are each a single cell. The egg is about the size of the smallest spot you can make on paper with a pencil point.

The nucleus of the sperm brings characteristics from the father and the nucleus of the egg contains characteristics from the mother (see pages 76 and 77).

Fertilized egg

Once fertilized, this one egg, small as it is, gives rise to all other tissues by repeated division.

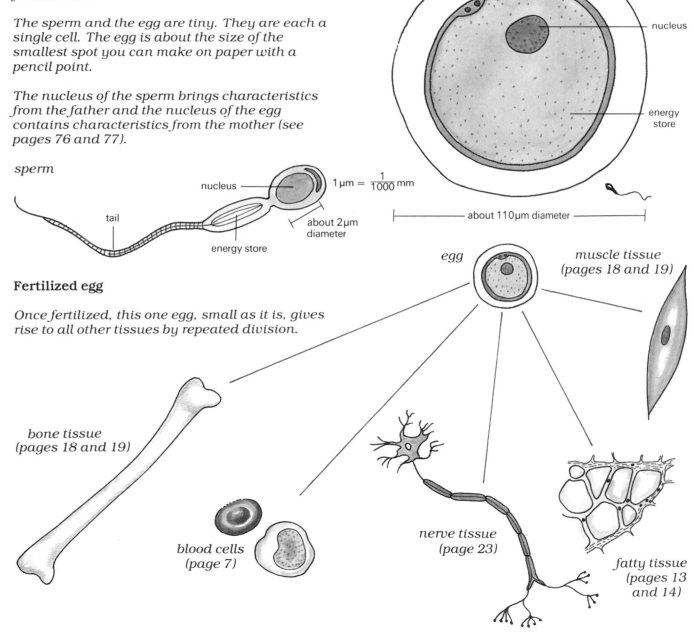

egg

nucleus

energy store

sperm

nucleus

tail

energy store

$1\,\mu m = \frac{1}{1000}\,mm$

about 2 µm diameter

about 110 µm diameter

egg

muscle tissue (pages 18 and 19)

bone tissue (pages 18 and 19)

blood cells (page 7)

nerve tissue (page 23)

fatty tissue (pages 13 and 14)

One aspect of reproduction which is of great interest to young children is the development of the baby in the womb from a tiny egg cell to a fully developed baby.

A full-size cut-out of a baby can be made and inserted into a body outline of a pregnant woman held on a pinboard.

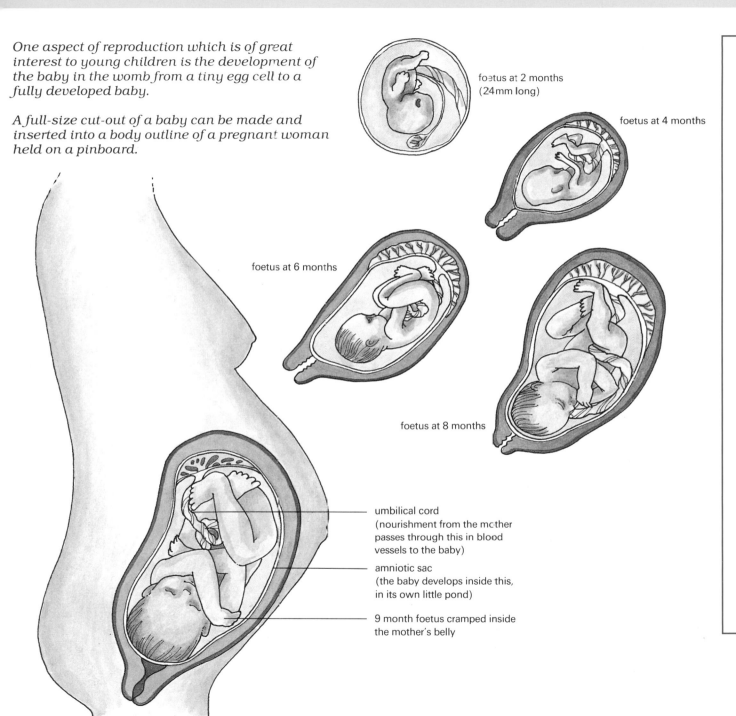

foetus at 2 months
(24mm long)

foetus at 4 months

foetus at 6 months

foetus at 8 months

umbilical cord
(nourishment from the mother passes through this in blood vessels to the baby)

amniotic sac
(the baby develops inside this, in its own little pond)

9 month foetus cramped inside the mother's belly

Sex education

There is a wide variety of 'standards' in society. Part of teaching is to help children come to some understanding of these 'standards' from the confusion in which they may find themselves.

Children come to school with a wide range of knowledge and beliefs. These beliefs are to be respected.

Children live under the influence of not only their families but also of their peer group and of the community in which they live. Their attempts to come to know themselves and others are important. Sex education needs to be put in a very wide context in which discussion plays a vital part.

The approach of this book, with its emphasis on life processes, provides one focus for discussion. Using it, one can study:
 human growth and change
 individual differences
 heredity
 reproduction.

However, there are other aspects which may well need to be knitted in with such a study:
 human feelings and moods
 gender conditioning
 peer-group pressure
 development of social skills.
A clear school policy on such issues helps.

TV

There are three sex-education programmes available from BBC TV:
 'Growing'
 'Someone new'
 'Life begins'

There is still a feeling that talk about smoking, drinking, glue sniffing and so on puts ideas into children's heads, but the reality is that children already have knowledge of such issues and are developing attitudes towards them from a young age.

These two pages give some information on drugs and suggest some approaches.

Alcohol

Alcohol is a depressant not a stimulant.

1 It causes us to be less inhibited. It may result in behaviour where we argue and insult people, or even fight them, all of which we may later regret.

2 Sends blood to the skin giving a feeling of warmth, which in reality results in a loss of body heat.

3 Causes our reactions to become slower, our speech slurred and our general body movements unsteady.

Alcohol is the most universally used of all drugs. The flow diagram below indicates some avenues for discussion and exploration.

Alcohol and different religions

Effect of alcohol on the body

Laws about alcohol

Exploring feelings and attitudes to alcohol

Places where alcohol is bought and sold

Use of alcohol in society

Drinks adults like, drinks children like

Smoking

Tobacco smoke contains nicotine which is absorbed through the lungs. It increases blood pressure and puts an increased load on the heart. Cancer and bronchitis are more common amongst smokers than non-smokers.

Here are some issues for discussion.

Should there be more non-smoking areas?

How advertisers make smoking look attractive

Discuss how nicotine is a habit forming drug

Interview smokers and list their reasons for smoking

Tobacco advertisers sponsoring sporting events

Interview non-smokers and gather their views about smoking

Cost of smoking

Fire hazards of smoking

Does smoking cause family rows?

What is the effect of smoking on body health?

School presentation

Devise a presentation on smoking for delivery at a school assembly. Prepare adverts, mock interviews and jingles.

The effects of habit-forming drugs fall into three broad groups: those that cause depression, stimulation and hallucination.

Depressants produce relaxation, and reduce the ability to think and act quickly.

Stimulants increase activity. The heart beats faster, alertness is increased and the need for food and sleep is reduced. Their danger lies in the dependence they cause, whereby people may cease to be alert unless they are under the influence of the drug.

Marijuana and LSD have well known hallucinogenic effects.

Habit-forming drugs produce *dependence* and *tolerance*.

Dependence

Dependence occurs when the user develops a need for the drug and the person's behaviour concentrates on satisfying this need.

If the person's body should become ill without the drug then *physical* dependence is established. Alcoholism is an example of this.

If withdrawal of the drug does not result in physical illness but the person suffers irritability and depression then a *psychic* dependence has been produced. Nicotine is an example of this.

Tolerance

Tolerance is when the body becomes used to the drug, and larger and larger doses are needed to give the same effect. Heroin produces tolerance very rapidly: it can take as little as three doses.

Discussion

Discussing and sharing information with children depends on the circumstances and attitudes of your school. However, all information must be reliable and all children need to be made aware of the dangers of drugs, especially of the more deadly ones.

They also need to be aware of those who supply drugs and their perniciousness in starting people on 'soft' drugs in order to convert them to 'hard' drugs later.

Medicines

Collect examples of medicines. Use magazines and the labels from medicine bottles and containers. Make a display.

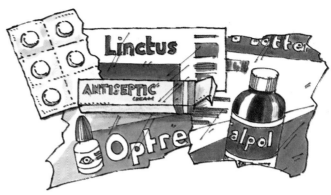

From such a display it is possible to enter into a discussion which emphasises the positive advantages that some drugs offer. This might be a good introduction into the whole issue of drugs.

Other things to do

List drugs and medicines commonly bought at the chemists and their purposes:
   asprin for pain relief
   cough medicine
   eye and ear drops
   ointments
   antacid for upset stomachs
   antiseptics.

Look at some medicine labels.

Stress the importance of following the instructions of either the label or a doctor.

Discuss:
   whether drugs are good or bad
   how drugs can be dangerous
   how drugs can be useful.

Some Common Drugs

Drug	Common forms	How taken	Effects
alcohol	beer, wines, spirits	drunk	depressant
nicotine	tobacco, cigarettes, cigars	smoked	stimulant
opium morphine heroin	morphine and heroin are opiates, that is derivatives of opium	smoked injected injected	depressant depressant depressant
cannabis	marijuana, or grass, is the leaves of the cannabis plant hash is cannabis resin	usually smoked mixed with tobacco	depressant, hallucinogen
barbiturates	sleeping tablets (sedatives)	pills/capsules	depressant
amphetamines	Benzedrine, speed, pep pills	pills/injected	stimulant, hallucinogen
cocaine	coke, snow, crack	snuff/injected	stimulant, hallucinogen
lysergic acid diethylamide	LSD, acid	pills/powder	hallucinogen

Respiration occurs in the tissues of plants and animals. It is the process by which they obtain energy.

Oxygen acts on sugars to release energy from them together with the gas carbon dioxide and water.

$$6O_2 + C_6H_{12}O_6 \longrightarrow 6CO_2 + 6H_2O + \text{energy}$$

(oxygen)   (sugar)   (carbon   (water)   dioxide)

Respiration is a continuous process. It occurs in both plants and animals throughout the day and night.

Plants and water

It can easily be shown that plants give off water.

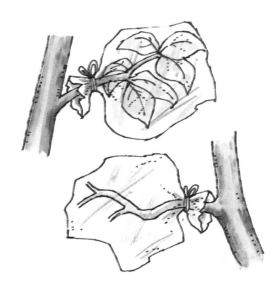

Tie a plastic bag firmly over the end of a leafy twig. Tie a second plastic bag firmly over a comparably sized twig that has been stripped of its leaves.

Compare the bags after 24 hours.

Plants and energy

Soak some pea seeds for 24 hours. Drain them and half fill a vacuum flask with them.

Record the temperature in the flask as the seeds germinate and grow. Hold the thermometer in place with cotton wool. This also seals the neck of the flask.

Use a second vacuum flask half full of dry pea seeds as a control.

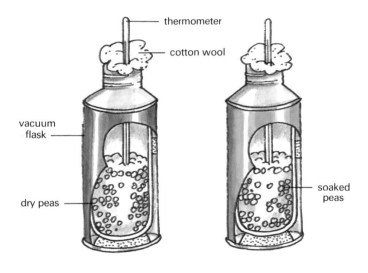

Check the temperature of each flask twice a day over a three-day period.

Day	Time	Temperature
1	9 am	
	3 pm	

To raise the temperature heat is needed. Heat is a form of energy. Not all the energy released by respiration is given off as heat. Some of it is stored in the seed and used for other processes.

Taking in oxygen

Plants and animals have to take in oxygen. In plants, the oxygen is taken from the air that enters the leaves through the pores in the leaves (stomata). These are found mainly on the undersurface of leaves.

In animals there are many mechanisms for taking up oxygen. That used in mammals is described on page 5. The following are brief descriptions of breathing mechanisms in some other animals.

Breathing in insects

Insects have small pores called spiracles on their bodies. These show up well, for example, in a caterpillar. The spiracles lead to delicate branching tubes which penetrate all parts of the body.

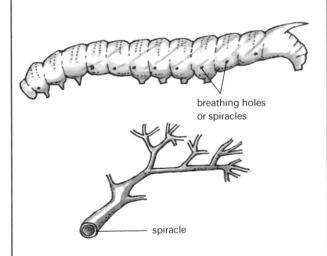

Thus, oxygen is taken directly to all parts of the body and not around in a blood stream.

The far ends of these branching tubes are moist. The oxygen dissolves in this moisture and is then taken up by the surrounding tissues.

Breathing in fish

In fish, water passes through the mouth and out through a series of gill slits. Soft feathery gills, which lie behind the gill slits, pick up oxygen from the water.

Some fish have a cover over the gill slits called an operculum. Other fish, like sharks and dogfish, do not have one.

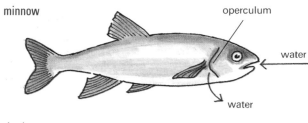

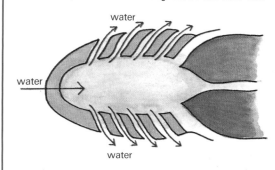

minnow

operculum

water

water

shark

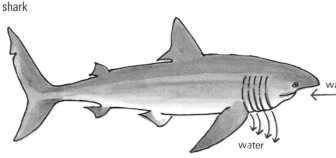

water

water

See 'An Early Start to Nature' (page 51) for experiments on fish breathing.

Breathing in snails

There is a breathing hole in the side of a snail. It leads into a cavity called the mantle cavity. This cavity has a moist lining which is rich in blood vessels.

Air is drawn in. Then the breathing hole closes. This increases the pressure in the cavity which facilitates the exchange of gases between the cavity and the blood vessels. Then the breathing hole opens and air is expelled.

breathing hole (pneumostome)

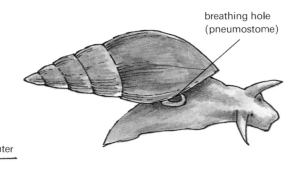

breathing hole (pneumostome)

'Breathing' is not as regular as in vertebrates and it may cease altogether when the snail hibernates.

Watch the opening. Time how often it opens and closes in 5 minutes.

Breathing in birds

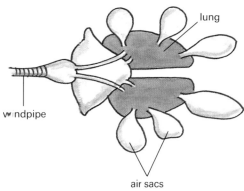

lung

windpipe

air sacs

Birds have lungs and a breathing mechanism similar to mammals, but they have no diaphragm. When air is breathed in it passes through the lungs and into special air sacs. It is these which increase and decrease in size with breathing, not the lungs.

The air thus passes through the lungs twice, once on breathing in and once on breathing out. This gives a very efficient uptake of oxygen.

Breathing in other animals

In earthworms oxygen dissolves in the moist coating on the outside of the worm.

Frogs take in oxygen through their moist skin (about half their oxygen is obtained in this way), through the lining of their mouth and through their lungs.

Photosynthesis is the process by which plants make food. In this process the energy from the sun is converted into a form which drives the whole of the living world.

Plants use carbon dioxide from the air and join this to water taken up through their roots to make sugars. Oxygen is formed as a by-product of the reaction and is given off into the air.

The process can only occur in sunlight (which provides the energy for the reaction) and in the presence of chlorophyll, the green colouring matter found in plants. Chlorophyll acts as a catalyst (an agent which speeds up a reaction but does not get used up during it).

$$6CO_2 + 6H_2O \xrightarrow[\text{chlorophyll}]{\text{sunlight}} C_6H_{12}O_6 + 6O_2$$

(carbon dioxide)   (water)   (sugar)   (oxygen)

The importance of this phenomenon cannot be overstressed. Herbivorous and carnivorous animals ultimately depend on it occurring.

Food chains

Make posters showing a variety of simple food chains. This will help show how plants, and hence photosynthesis, are essential to life.

Show that a gas is given off

It is easy to demonstrate that a gas is given off in photosynthesis using Canadian pondweed. This is common in ponds and canals, or can be bought from garden centres.

Put some pondweed under a clear funnel in a bowl of water. Fill a medicine bottle with water and invert it over the funnel.

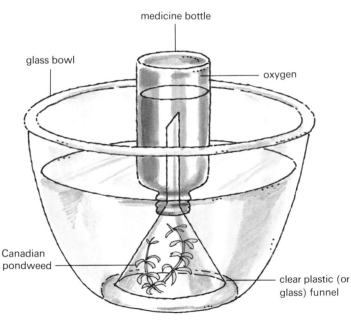

medicine bottle

glass bowl

oxygen

Canadian pondweed

clear plastic (or glass) funnel

As the pondweed photosynthesises it will give off a gas (oxygen), which will collect in the top of the medicine bottle. Make sure you set it up in bright sunlight.

Plant growth and sunlight

The effect of sunlight on growing plants is easy to demonstrate.

Germinate three bean seeds, each in a separate pot containing the same type of compost. Put one on a bright, sunny windowsill in the classroom, one in a darkish corner and the third in a cupboard.

on a sunny windowsill

in a dark corner of the classroom

in a cupboard

The plant on the sunny windowsill will grow normally as will the plant in a darkish corner, although the one in the sunlight will be healthier and stronger. The plant in the cupboard will be etiolated. That is, it will be thin and straggly, and lack colour.

When insects visit a flower they pick up pollen from the anthers of the stamens. As they move about they may brush this pollen onto the stigma, or they may fly to another flower and brush off pollen onto the stigma of this flower. This is *pollination*.

The pollen grains stick to the stigma of the flower. A pollen tube grows down from each pollen grain to each ovule in the ovary. The male nucleus in the pollen grain passes down the pollen tube to fuse with the female nucleus in the ovule. This fusion is *fertilization*.

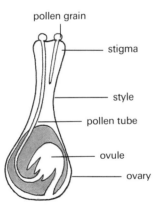

pollen grain
stigma
style
pollen tube
ovule
ovary

The fertilized ovule grows into a seed. The ovary grows into the fruit.

You may, for example, when shelling pea pods (the fruit of the pea) find some ovules that have not been fertilized and hence have not grown into seeds.

Flowers

The structure of flowers, and activities to carry out with flowers, are fully described in 'An Early Start to Nature'. Flowers are there for the reproduction of the plant.

Seeds and growth

Soak some seeds and set them to grow.

Mustard and cress will grow quickly. Bean and sunflower seeds can both be grown right through to maturity. The whole cycle from seed to plant to flower to fruit and seed can then be studied at first hand.

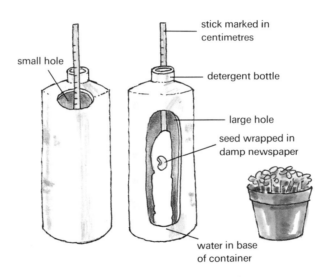

small hole

stick marked in centimetres

detergent bottle

large hole

seed wrapped in damp newspaper

water in base of container

Dissect the soaked seed to examine the various parts.

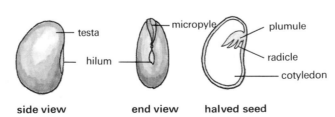

testa

hilum

micropyle

plumule

radicle

cotyledon

side view   **end view**   **halved seed**

Make drawings as the seeds grow.

French bean seed

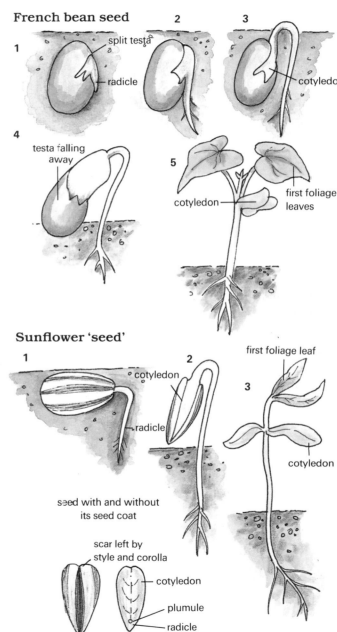

1   2   3

split testa

radicle

cotyledon

4

testa falling away

5

cotyledon

first foliage leaves

Sunflower 'seed'

first foliage leaf

1   2   3

cotyledon

radicle

seed with and without its seed coat

cotyledon

scar left by style and corolla

cotyledon

plumule

radicle

Movement in animals is an obvious thing to watch and study. Movement is often in response to some stimulus.

Human movement

Make a cardboard figure with stiff limbs.

Tie coloured PE bands to arms and legs of a child. Red bands to right limbs, blue bands to left limbs.

paper fastener

paper fastener

Ask the child to move slowly.

Discuss the sequence of movements. Copy them using the cardboard model. Work out the sequence.

Note how the body is constantly moved forward yet kept upright with the main body mass roughly in the centre. This helps us to keep in balance.

Movement in other animals

Insects

Look at how a beetle moves, although you will need a very slow moving beetle to see its movement clearly.

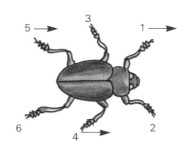 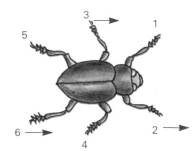

Insects move legs 1, 4 and 5 together while balancing on their remaining legs. Legs 2, 3 and 6 then move together.

Worms

Observe the movement of a worm.

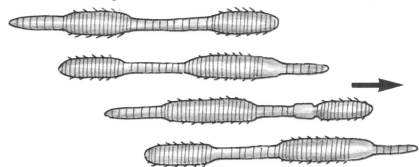

Muscles running around the worm contract to make the worm long and thin. Muscles running the length of the worm contract to make it short and fat.

Long thin segments have their bristles withdrawn. Short fat segments have their bristles out anchoring the worm.

Snails

Snails move on a single muscular foot. Bands of muscular movement ripple along the foot.

clear plastic sheet

If you look carefully you can count the muscle bands.

Other animals

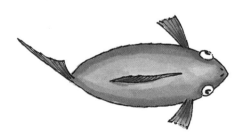

For movement in fish and other animals, as well as response of these animals to stimuli, see 'An Early Start to Nature' (pages 36–47, 50, 51), where there are many suggestions for practical activities.

Birds

footprints of a bird that hops

footprints of a bird that walks

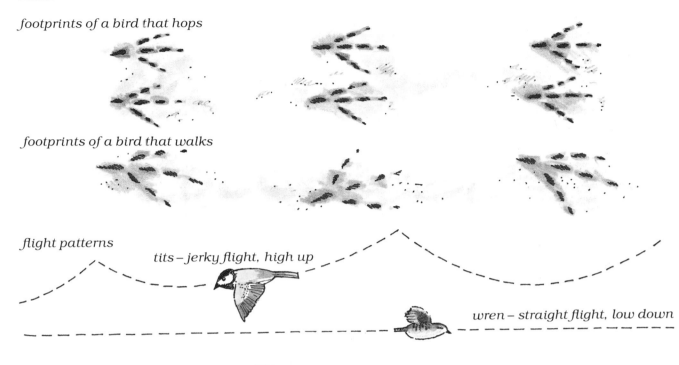

flight patterns

tits – jerky flight, high up

wren – straight flight, low down

thrush – a bounding flight

Plant movements

Plants show growth movements in response to light, water and gravity. See 'An Early Start to Nature' (page 27) for suggestions on what to do.

Nastic movements

Daisies close up in the evening and open again in the daylight. The leaves of clover show similar nastic movements.

This is a very brief outline of Darwin's work and theory in order to provide a background that illustrates why developing the concept of variation with primary school children is important.

Charles Darwin (1809–1882) was not outstandingly successful at school, although he came from a family of exceptional ability. On leaving school he went to Edinburgh University to study medicine but found he couldn't stand the sight of blood and left to take a degree at Cambridge.

He was destined for a life in the Church, but by chance was recommended by the botanist Professor Henslow to serve as a naturalist on HMS Beagle, which was about to set out on a world tour.

It is as well to remember that Darwin set out on this voyage with a background not only of his work at university but also of a family interested in the natural world and in evolution.

Indeed, his grandfather Erasmus Darwin had written in *Zoonomia*: 'From this account of reproduction it appears that all animals share a similar origin, viz from a single living filament.'

During the voyage Darwin noted a number of things:

1 He found many fossils and was struck by their similarity to present-day creatures.

For example, fossil remains of glyptodon in South America are very similar to the modern-day armadillos.

glyptodon

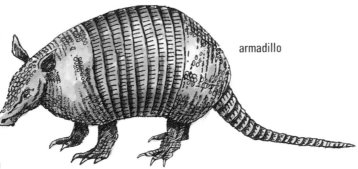

armadillo

This shows there is a relationship between the animals of the past and those now living.

2 He noted the relationship between animals and plants of South America and those of Africa and Australia.

For example, there is the South American rhea, African ostrich and the Australian emu. They are all similar and form a distinct group of birds.

rhea

ostrich

emu

Darwin suggested that the difference between them had arisen because of their life in different environments. In past ages they had a common ancestor from which a number of varieties arose.

By their physical separation, because of mountain ranges, seas and sheer distance, those varieties best suited to the prevailing environmental conditions survived.

These animals became so different from the 'relatives' they were separated from that they could no longer interbreed with them and so a new species was formed.

3 During his voyage on HMS Beagle, Darwin went to the Galapagos Islands where he found many animals that live only on those islands.

The carefulness of some of his observations is shown in his study of the finches found on the island. There were fourteen species, each with its own characteristics.

The finches:
(a) are only found in the Galapagos islands
(b) show similarities to birds on the South American mainland which is the nearest landmass
(c) on some islands are confined to that one island even though the islands are near to each other.

Darwin suggested that his fourteen species of finch had arisen from a mainland species of finch which had come to the islands. The physical barriers of sea and distance, coupled with time, had resulted in varieties better suited to the conditions on the islands.

These in turn became better suited to the differing conditions on each island and took to breeding only with birds very like themselves. Thus new species arose.

Darwin on his return wrote:

'These facts … seemed to throw some light on the origin of species – that mystery of mysteries, as it has been called by one of our greatest philosophers.

'On my return home, it occurred to me, in 1837, that something might be made out of this question by patiently accumulating and reflecting on all sorts of facts which could possibly have any bearing on it.

medium ground finch

large insectivorous tree finch

cactus ground finch

warbler finch

'After five years of work, I allowed myself to speculate on the subject and drew up some short notes, these I enlarged into a sketch of the conclusions, which then seemed probable: from that period to the present day I have steadily pursued the same object.'

From all his studies and thinking Darwin wrote his now famous book *On the Origin of Species by Means of Natural Selection, or the Preservation of Favoured Races in the Struggle for Life*. In this book he presented an overwhelming collection of evidence from fossil and other sources that life had evolved from forms living in the past.

This idea was not new, for his grandfather, among others, had made the same suggestion. However, no one before had brought so much evidence to support the suggestion.

What was new was that Darwin proposed a theory – a mechanism to suggest what brought such evolution about.

It consists essentially of three facts and two deductions.

1 There is a tendency for the numbers of all organisms to increase geometrically.

2 Yet numbers are usually constant.
[*There is therefore a struggle for existence* – first deduction.]

3 There is variation between individuals, some being better adapted than others.
[*Therefore there will be natural selection* – second deduction.]

Thus variation is inherited and in generation after generation those variations best suited for survival persist.

This is at the heart of Darwin's theory, and so it is vital to build up the concept of variation when teaching young children.

It is interesting and valuable to describe to the older juniors the times in which Charles Darwin was putting forward his theory of evolution by natural selection.

They were very different times from today. Religion played a very prominent role in society and most Christians took every word in the Bible as true.

The Book of Genesis was taken as fact. God had created the world in six days and all the creatures of the earth had sprung into life at the same moment. Indeed they had only survived because Noah had taken a male and female of each species into the ark.

Such beliefs are held by people today, but in Victorian times they were at the heart of society and to remove them was to threaten the very social order that bound people together.

The Church was aroused and, led by the redoubtable Samuel Wilberforce, Bishop of Oxford, assembled at Oxford in June 1860 to debate the issue at a meeting of the British Association. It was a famous meeting: the foremost scientists and the foremost churchmen debating Darwin's theory on the origin of species.

Bishop Wilberforce was an eloquent speaker, too eloquent for some, for his nickname was Soapy Sam. During the course of his peroration he turned to T.H. Huxley in the audience to make his now well known query: 'Was it through his grandfather or his grandmother that he claimed descent from a monkey?'

To which we have Huxley's breathtaking reply: 'I asserted — and I repeat — that a man has no reason to be ashamed of having an ape for his grandfather.

'If there was an ancestor whom I should feel shame in recalling, it would rather be a man, a man of restless and versatile intellect, who, not content with an unequivocal success in his own sphere of activity, plunges into scientific questions with which he has no real acquaintance, only to obscure them by aimless rhetoric, and distract the attention of his hearers from the real point at issue by eloquent digressions and skilled appeals to religious prejudice.'

Some animals, like the dinosaurs, became extinct many millions of years ago (page 69). Others, like the marsupial wolf (or Tasmanian tiger), have become extinct much more recently.

The giant tortoise and iguana were two of the animals that Charles Darwin observed during his voyage.

marsupial wolf

giant tortoise

iguana

It is well to point out to children, for they too often misunderstand, that Darwin never claimed man's descent from monkeys. What he really said was that man and apes both had a common ancestor in the past and that each proceeded along its own evolutionary pathway.

The caricatures on the opposite page are of Samuel Wilberforce, T.H. Huxley and Charles Darwin and were drawn by 'Ape' for the magazine *Vanity Fair*.

Samuel Wilberforce

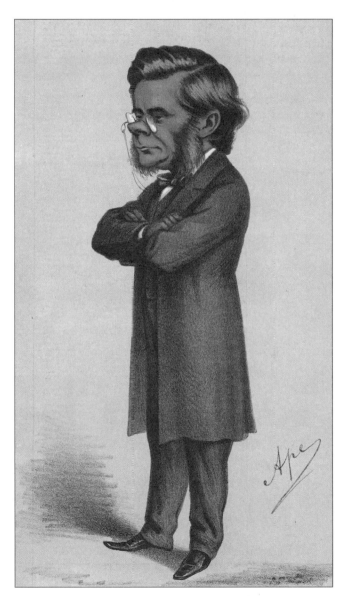

T. H. Huxley

Charles Darwin

One of the most important concepts to develop with children is that of variation. It is essential to any eventual understanding of Darwin's theory of evolution by natural selection.

Although Darwin's theory is one that most primary-school children will probably only come to fully understand at a much later stage of their development (when well into their secondary school programme of work), the idea of variation is one that they can grasp.

It has to be built up continually through their primary school life from many examples.

For example, studying trees illustrates the great variation there is in tree leaves, both in colour and shape, as is so clearly illustrated on the opposite page.

Examples in variation in ourselves and practical exploration of such variations are given on pages 58–61.

It is surprising how often the concept comes into general classroom work, but it is also important to make it explicit to children.

Variation in the banded snail (*Cepaea nemoralis*)

Variation in the human race

Variation in leaves

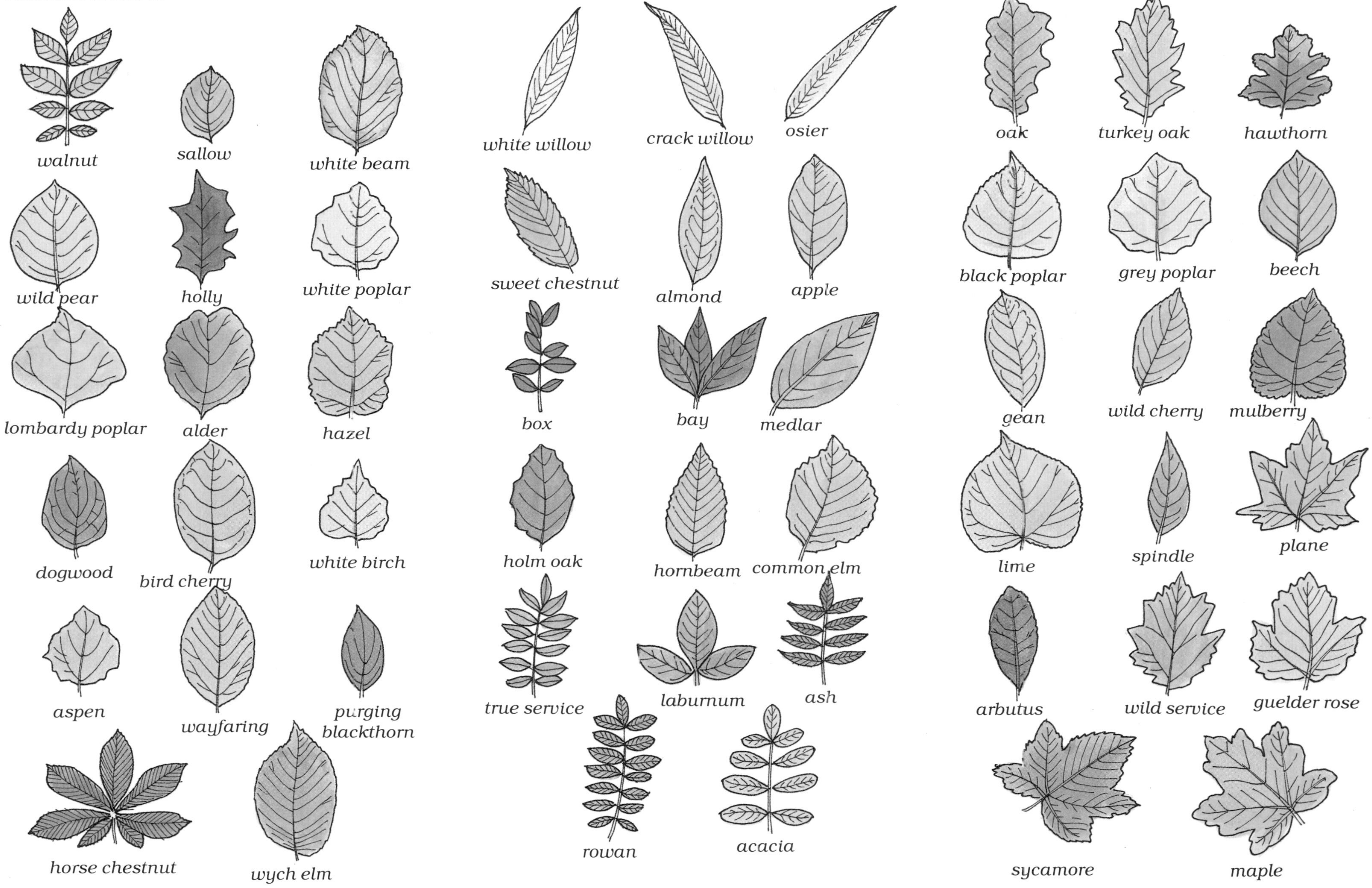

walnut

sallow

white beam

white willow

crack willow

osier

oak

turkey oak

hawthorn

wild pear

holly

white poplar

sweet chestnut

almond

apple

black poplar

grey poplar

beech

lombardy poplar

alder

hazel

box

bay

medlar

gean

wild cherry

mulberry

dogwood

bird cherry

white birch

holm oak

hornbeam

common elm

lime

spindle

plane

aspen

wayfaring

purging blackthorn

true service

laburnum

ash

arbutus

wild service

guelder rose

horse chestnut

wych elm

rowan

acacia

sycamore

maple

There are lots of body variations in a class of children. These are some that can be measured.

Height

sitting  *standing*

Mass

Circumference of waist

Head circumference

Hand measurements

hand area

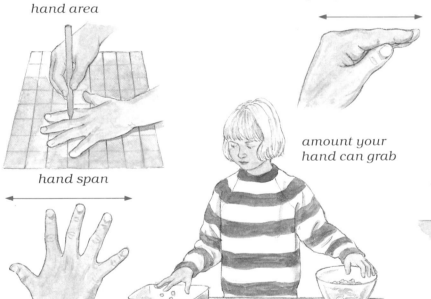

hand span

Foot measurements

length

area

length of middle finger

width 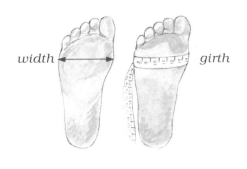 *girth*

amount your hand can grab

volume of your hand by immersion in water

Also

You can also measure:
circumference of chest (see page 5)
area of body silhouette (see page 20)

Name	Height	Height sitting	Mass	Circumference of			Length of middle finger		Hand								Foot								Area of silhouette
				head	chest	waist			span		area		volume		grab		length		width		area		girth		
							L	R	L	R	L	R	L	R	L	R	L	R	L	R	L	R	L	R	

These are some body variations that can be recorded or talked about.

Foot shapes

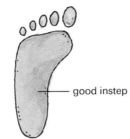

good instep

Noses

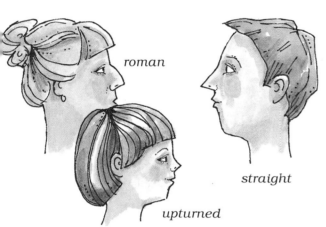

roman

upturned

straight

Profile silhouettes

Draw round the shadow. Cut it out to make a profile silhouette.

Tongues

folded down the centre

folded back on itself

Ear lobes

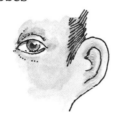

fixed to head

free

Hair colours

ginger

blonde

black

Hair type

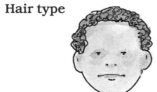

curly

straight

Eye colours *(see page 24)*

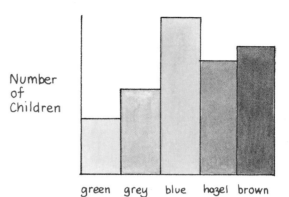

Number of Children

green | grey | blue | hazel | brown

Face shapes

heart shaped

round

oblong

oval

square

triangular

Fingerprints *(see page 21)*

loops

whorl

arch

composite

We all know whether we are right or left handed, but do we always favour this dominant aspect of our behaviour? Do we sometimes show an asymmetry in our actions?

Fold hands interlocking fingers

Do this quickly.

How many children put right thumb over left thumb?

How many children put left thumb over right thumb?

Clap hands

Which hand is on top?

Hold your hands behind your back

Which hand does the holding?

Scratch the centre of your back

Which hand does the scratching?

Cup your ear to catch a sound better

Which ear do you cup?

Fold your arms

Do you put your right arm over left, or left over right?

Wink at someone

Are you a right-eyed or left-eyed winker?

Tilt your head on your shoulder

Which shoulder does your head touch?

Dominant eye

Point at an object across the room with your index finger, say a book on a shelf. Close your right eye. Open it. Close your left eye.

When you close one of your eyes, the object will appear to jump to one side. This closed eye is your dominant eye. When you close your other eye, the object will be lined up with your dominant eye.

Count to five on one hand

Use the index finger of one hand on the other.

Which index finger do you use?

Further activities

Count up the number of left-sided and the number of right-sided features for each child in the class. Look for any patterns in the individual columns.

For example, the population is strongly biased towards right handedness, but is this true for all traits?

See if children can suggest other things to try. Crossing legs, twitching an eyebrow and waving are three more.

Name	Thumb test	Clapping hand	Scratching back	Holding hand behind back	Folding arms	Cupping ear	Winking	Head tilting	Counting	Pointing	Total	
											R	L
John Jones	left	right	left	right	right	right	right	left	right	right		
Kusuma Barnett	left	left	right	right	right	left	left	left	left	right		

Fossils are the remains of plants or animals that have turned to stone. They are almost always evidence of the hard parts of organisms that lived in the past. It is things such as bones, shells and teeth of animals or the trunks, branches and leaves of trees that tend to become fossilised. The soft parts were inevitably subject to rapid decay by bacterial agents and did not survive long enough to be fossilised.

How are fossils formed?

By alteration

Many fossils are formed by water gradually breaking down the hard materials left by an animal to leave a light, spongy structure. This is filled by chemicals from the soil, which harden to form a fossil.

An ammonite where the original shell has been replaced by iron pyrites.

By burying in amber

The hard outer covering or exoskeleton of an insect is sometimes found intact in the hardened resin of trees, which forms amber.

By moulds and casts

1 An animal, say a snail, dies and is buried in sand. The body rots leaving the shell.

2 The shell slowly dissolves in chemicals from the sand, leaving a cavity. The wall of the cavity has an identical shape and texture to that of the shell. It becomes a mould.

3 Chemicals dissolved in the sand percolate into the mould, harden and form a cast.

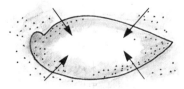

4 If the mould and the cast are carefully separated, you end up with a fossil mould and a fossil cast.

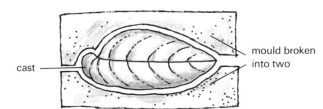

cast

mould broken into two

How are fossils retrieved?

Palaeontologists recover fossils in a number of basic ways.

By drilling

A drill, rather like that used by a dentist, is used to delicately remove the rock.

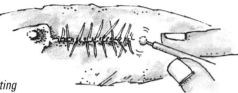

By sand blasting

This only works if the fossil is harder than the rock in which it is embedded. The grit wears away the softer rock.

By washing down

If the fossils are embedded in soft rock such as chalk then the chalk can be washed away because it is so soft.

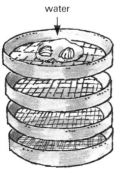

water

series of sieves to capture tiny fossils

By bathing in acid

This is used to remove fossils embedded in limestone.

Making moulds and casts

Method 1

Cuttlefish bone, which is sold by pet shops for birds, is ideal for making a mould.

1 Cut a piece of cuttlefish bone in two.

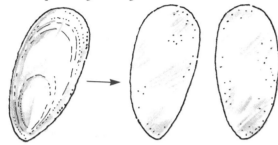

2 Press a shell between the two halves.

3 Remove the shell.

4 Carefully put the two halves of the bone back together to form the mould.

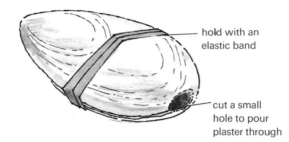

hold with an elastic band

cut a small hole to pour plaster through

5 Mix some plaster of Paris (dental plaster is best) by adding the plaster powder to the water. Stir continuously until the mixture is the consistency of double cream. Straightaway pour it into the mould. Make sure it is well packed down.

Tap the sides of the mould gently to remove air bubbles, as these would weaken the cast.

6 When the plaster has set, remove the two halves of the mould to obtain your 'fossil' cast.

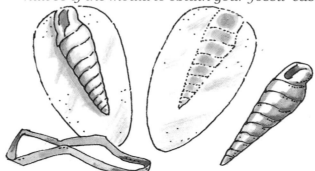

Method 2

The traditional method of making plaster casts of twigs or animal footprints (see 'An Early Start to Nature', page 7) can also be used for making 'fossil casts'.

1 Put some damp sand into the bottom of a discarded aluminium-foil food tray. Press in a shell to make a mould.

2 Mix some plaster of Paris. Pour it without delay into the mould. Leave to set.

3 Remove the cast. Paint it using realistic colours against a contrasting background.

Many fossil footprints have been discovered. Indeed, some prehistoric animals are known only from their footprints.

An animal would walk along, say, in the soft mud on a river bank leaving its footprints. These would bake in the sun to form moulds. These moulds in turn would fill with mud and form fossils as described on page 62.

Protoceratops
1.5–2 metres long

Make your own footprint trail

1 You can use powder paint. Cover the floor with newspaper. Have water in a washing-up bowl and a towel to clean the feet afterwards. Make prints by walking along a line of kitchen paper.

2 Try using talcum powder. Make prints by walking along sheets of black sugar paper stuck together with masking tape.

3 Draw round feet as a child advances slowly along the reverse side of a roll of wallpaper.

Make some dinosaur footprints. Draw one on card to begin with. Cut it out and use it as a template to make lots of footprints. Use newspaper or magazine pages so that you can easily make a lot at once.

Lay a trail of footprints along the corridor and through the school hall. Outdoors you can chalk around card templates on the playground.

Try to judge the distance apart of the footprints. The sizes of some dinosaurs are given on this page as a yardstick to judge by.

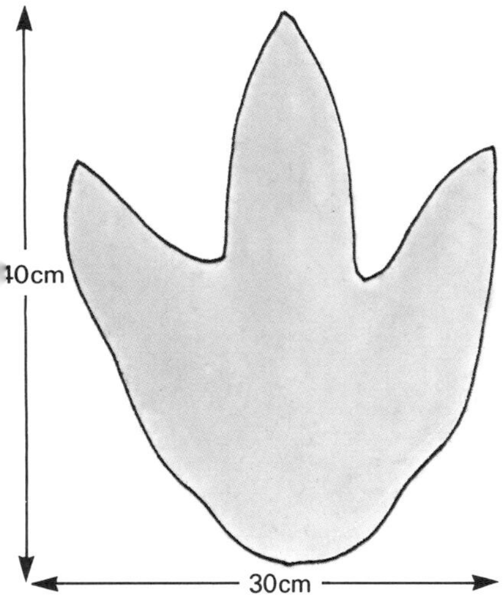

40cm

30cm

▼**Stegosaurus**
This was about 7–9 metres long.

▼**Tyrannosaurus**
The largest carnivorous dinosaur known. It was about 18 metres long.

▼**Coelophysis**
This was up to 1.5 metres long. Coelophysis may have used its long fingers to grasp its prey. It was one of the earliest dinosaurs.

▼**Triceratops**
One of the most recent dinosaurs. They died out about 65 million years ago. They were about 14 metres long.

▲**Diplodocus**
These were the real giants, up to 27 metres long. They were plant eaters.

Remember that even though a human figure is shown to indicate scale, there were no people around. Dinosaurs existed over 200 million years ago and died out about 60 million years ago. Our ancestors came along about one million years ago.

A pictorial representation of a scene from a past age can easily be created with cut out figures arranged against a painted backdrop.

This helps children to imagine what life in the past was like, and sets them into researching what animals and plants lived together at a particular period in time. They also need to find the size of organisms in order to get a rough idea of scale for a scene.

Here are two examples.

Remember when painting the backdrop for this scene from the Cretaceous period that this was the age of fern-like plants and trees. Modern flowering plants as we know them were only just beginning to appear in primitive forms.

Use a card tab stuck behind each animal to hold it up.

1 Tyrannosaurus was a great meat eater. It had long dagger-like teeth up to 15 centimetres long.

2 Triceratops was a plant eater. It had a great bony frill above its head for protection.

3 Styracosaurus was another plant eater. It had a mass of horns above its head for protection.

4 Ornithomimus was one of the 'ostrich' dinosaurs.

5 Deinonychus was a meat eater. It was just over 2 metres high.

folded card

This diorama shows a sea scene in Triassic/ Jurassic times.

The cut-out animals are suspended by cotton threads from a shoe box placed on its side.

The inside of the shoe box is coloured blue and the base yellow. Sprinkle the base with sand and either a few seeds or some gravel to simulate the sea bed.

1 Ichthyosaurus, a 'fish-lizard', was about 3 metres long. They hunted in packs feeding on belemnites, squid-like creatures.

2 Plesiosaurus, another carnivore, was 3.5–7 metres long.

3 Archelon was a huge turtle up to 4 metres long.

4 Cryptoclidus was 3 metres long. It is another plesiosaur. Some people think that 'Nessie', the Loch Ness Monster, is one.

5 Placodus was a shell-eating marine reptile about 2 metres long.

6 Belemnite was a squid-like animal.

Young children are fascinated by fossils and any collection will usually arouse much enthusiasm.

It is important to have some good secondary-source books, not only to identify the fossils, but to find out when the animals lived, how they lived and what other animals were around at the time.

For this last purpose it is of great help if you can obtain a piece of rock containing three or four different fossils so that you can show them existing together.

The corals in the piece of limestone on the right indicate that there were once warm seas covering Shropshire.

A trilobite was a prehistoric creature related to the woodlouse. It was a bottom-feeding scavenger picking up scraps from the sea bed. Its flattened body with eyes on the top surface and the mandibles on the lower surface for breaking up food suggest this mode of life.

Brachiopods are two-valued animals rather like a cockle with the hard shells protecting a soft body. One shell is slightly larger than the other.

Brachiopods

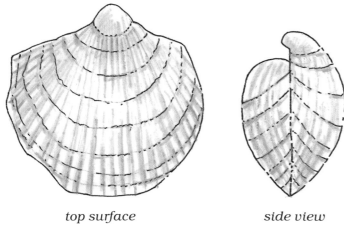

top surface   side view

limestone from Wenlock Edge, Shropshire

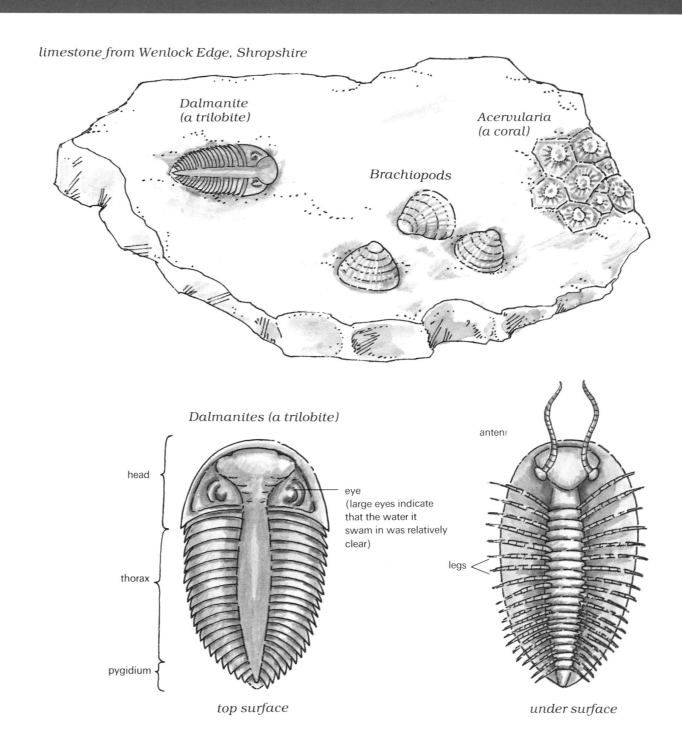

Dalmanites (a trilobite)

head
thorax
pygidium

eye
(large eyes indicate that the water it swam in was relatively clear)

top surface

anten

legs

under surface

Children develop a concept of time slowly. Even fairly recent history, such as the Elizabethans and the Stuarts, is for many children nothing more than story telling. It is an even more difficult task to put the animals of prehistoric times into some kind of historical perspective.

The following activities will help give children an understanding of the time span involved.

My time line

Ask children to make a time line of their own life. Each interval represents one year.

Age	
1	walked
2	
3	caught measles
4	sister born
5	went to school
6	learnt to read
7	went to Majorca
8	broke collar bone
9	
10	in school team which won the cup
11	now

Make a historical time line

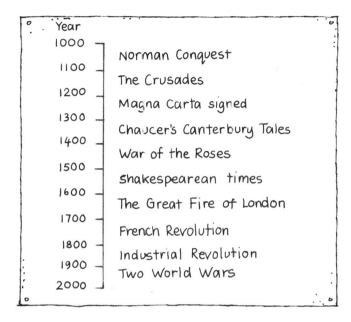

Year	
1000	
1100	Norman Conquest
1200	The Crusades
	Magna Carta signed
1300	Chaucer's Canterbury Tales
1400	War of the Roses
1500	Shakespearean times
1600	The Great Fire of London
1700	French Revolution
1800	Industrial Revolution
1900	Two World Wars
2000	

Make an inventions time line

1300	spectacles
1450	printing
1530	spinning wheel
1657	vacuum pump (Otto von Guericke)
1712	steam engine (Thomas Newcomen)
1768	steam engine (James Watt)
1769	Spinning Jenny (Richard Arkwright)
1796	vaccination
1831	dynamo (Michael Faraday)
1837	telegraph
1839	photography
1846	anaesthesia
1858	Atlantic cable
1868	antiseptic surgery
1876	telephone
1903	aeroplane (Wright Bros.)
1945	atomic bomb
1947	Polaroid camera

Geological time

A number of makes of toilet roll have over 280 sheets. Use two rolls and let each sheet represent 1 million years. Unroll the paper and run it down the corridor, through the hall and so on until you have over 500 million years spread before you.

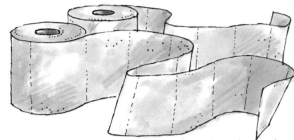

Make pictures of prehistoric animals. Then place them at appropriate points along your time scale.

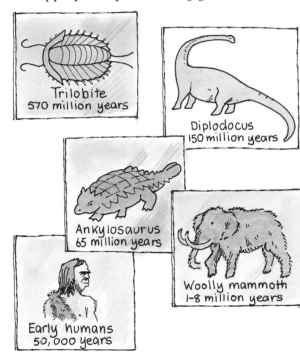

Trilobite
570 million years

Diplodocus
150 million years

Ankylosaurus
65 million years

Woolly mammoth
1–8 million years

Early humans
50,000 years

The appearance of human beings very recently (yesterday so to speak) becomes apparent.

The development of the horse from a tiny creature the size of a poodle and with toed feet, who browsed on forest leaves, to the present-day horse, a graceful animal that walks on single toes and feeds on grassland is a useful one to follow with children.

It presents a comprehensive picture of development through different forms. It needs to be prefaced by a consideration of the typical mammalian limb, the so-called pentadactyl limb.

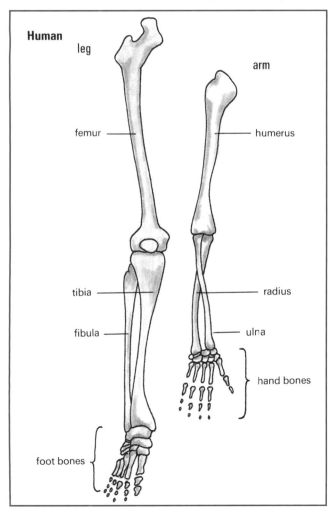

Human

leg

arm

femur

humerus

tibia

radius

fibula

ulna

hand bones

foot bones

Make a plan as shown below. Use thin, coloured strips of sticky paper.

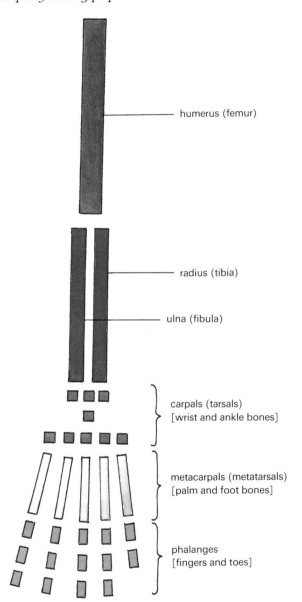

humerus (femur)

radius (tibia)

ulna (fibula)

carpals (tarsals)
[wrist and ankle bones]

metacarpals (metatarsals)
[palm and foot bones]

phalanges
[fingers and toes]

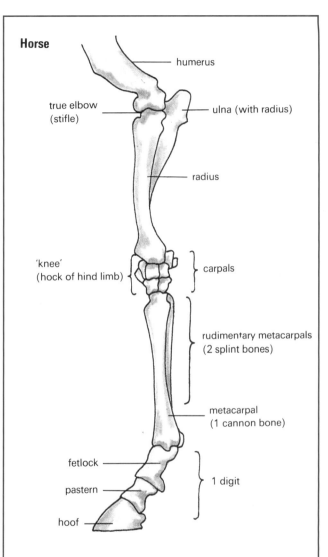

Horse

humerus

true elbow
(stifle)

ulna (with radius)

radius

'knee'
(hock of hind limb)

carpals

rudimentary metacarpals
(2 splint bones)

metacarpal
(1 cannon bone)

fetlock

1 digit

pastern

hoof

The typical mammalian limb shown of humans is considerably modified in the horse.

The upper-arm bone (humerus) and the lower-arm bone (radius) are easily recognisable. Also one of the bones of the palm (metacarpal) is considerably elongated. It ends attached to one digit. A horse literally walks on its fingers. The hoof is the nail of the finger.

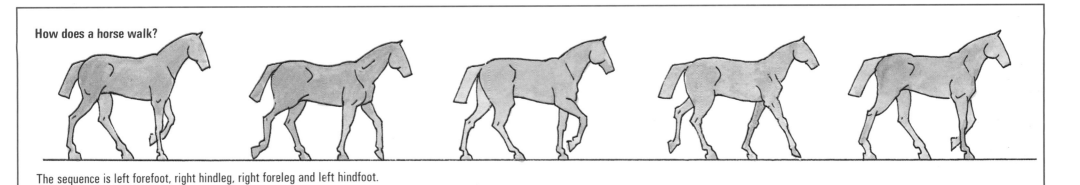

How does a horse walk?

The sequence is left forefoot, right hindleg, right foreleg and left hindfoot.

Walk like a horse

Line up two children to mimic a walking horse.

1 *The 'front legs' puts his or her right foot forward then the 'rear legs' puts his or her left foot forward.*

2 *The 'front legs' puts his or her left foot forward then the 'rear legs' puts his or her right foot forward.*

3 *Repeat the steps.*

Ask the 'horse' to walk along a roll of kitchen paper or the back of a wallpaper roll.

Quickly mark each 'footprint' with a pencilled cross. Print hoof marks onto the pencilled crosses with a large potato-cut of a hoof.

Look for hoof prints

unshod horse
(over 11.5 cm across)

shod horse

See 'An Early Start to Nature' (page 56).

'front legs'

'hindlegs'

potato-cut 'hoof'

ink pad

It is tempting to form fossil remains of horses into one evolutionary chain with one species evolving from another. However, our records would have to be immensely comprehensive to be able to do this and the fossil record only shows us snapshots at various times through the past.

Palaeontologists make intelligent guesses at evolutionary lives from the evidence they have gathered. Some of the horses might have given rise to the next horse in the sequence, some of them might not.

Hyracotherium (Eohippus) – 60 million years ago

This tiny creature, about the size of a small poodle, stood about 28 centimetres high and lived 60 000 000 years ago in Eocene forests.

The forests were full of tropical trees and it is reasonable to suggest that Hyracotherium browsed on the low lying leaves because it had low-crowned flat teeth.

It ran on its toes which had toenails but not hooves. It was probably very good at leaping over fallen branches and squeezing through gaps to get away from enemies.

Feet: four toes on the front feet, three toes on the rear feet.
Teeth: small, low crowned with a difference in size between the molars and premolars.

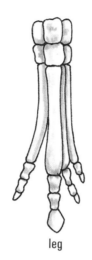

leg

Mesohippus – 35 million years ago

Mesohippus lived in the Oligocene period about 35 000 000 years ago.

It was about the size of a sheep. The premolar and molar teeth were a similar size, which indicates it had become better at grinding vegetation.

Like Hyracotherium it was a forest dweller and it had feet very like those of a dog.

Feet: three toes on each foot.
Teeth: premolar and molar teeth similar in size with a pattern of ridges for grinding food.

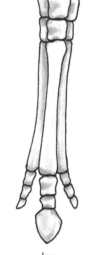

leg

Merychippus – 20 million years ago

Merychippus lived in the Miocene period about 20 000 000 years ago. By this time the grasses had evolved forming great plains and Merychippus had adapted to feeding on grass.

Thus the horse had evolved from a browser to a grazer. The teeth were strong and high crowned to withstand the constant grinding of grass.

Merychippus walked on the tips of its toes. Although it had three toes on each foot the central toe was enlarged and it really ran on one toe on each foot. This made it a speedy animal.

Feet: three toes on each foot but the central toe enlarged and elongated.
Teeth: high crowned and made of dentine, enamel and cement.

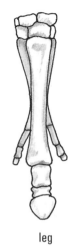

leg

Equus – 3 million years ago to the present day

The modern horse is an efficient grazer and is built for speed.

The leg (see also page 70) concentrates down onto a single elongated digit with the toe shod with a large hoof which is an adapted toenail. The foot bones have been reduced to tiny splints.

With eyes set well back on the head it has a wide field of vision. Its large brain makes it an intelligent animal.

Feet: one elongated toe with the toenail forming the hoof.
Teeth: open-rooted grinders.

leg

Peppered moth – *Biston betularia*

Normal form (white form)

Melanic form, variety carbonaria (black form)

actual size

It is rare to find examples of evolution in action because the process is so long and drawn out. It is usually measured in countless thousands of years.

An interesting example of evolution actually in action today over a relatively small time scale is presented by the peppered moth.

In its normal form it is mottled black and white. This is the so-called white form. During the last 150 years a melanic form has appeared which is dark in colour, the so-called black form.

This form is protectively coloured in smoke-blackened industrial regions. In Manchester during the latter half of the nineteenth century it increased enormously in relation to the number of white forms.

It was thought that the advent of the Industrial Revolution and the subsequent grime in the environment provided a background with which the black form merged better than its white counterpart. Thus it was less likely to be eaten by predators.

In the 1950s, a brilliant series of controlled experiments by Professor Kettlewell established that this was so. He released both white and black forms in both industrial and rural surroundings and then compared the numbers of black and white moths recaptured.

The main predators of the moth are birds. In an industrial area more white forms of the peppered moths were eaten than black forms. Conversely, in rural areas more black forms were taken than white forms.

This is an example of animal camouflage and an example of survival of the fittest. Intriguingly the black form is now becoming common in some rural areas, which suggests it has some other advantages over the white form.

You can play an interesting and informative game by drawing and cutting out some peppered moths, both white and black forms, and hiding them against light and dark backgrounds.

A group of children can set up the test. They can then test the rest of the class to see how many moths they can spot.

1 Begin by making some bark rubbings.

Pin a large sheet of white paper to a tree and rub it with candle wax. The candle wax will pick out the ridges in the bark. Do the same with a second sheet.

candle

Colour one sheet with a black paint wash to simulate dark grimy bark. Colour the other sheet with a light yellow/white wash to simulate light-coloured bark. Add some little patches of brown to make it look more realistic.

2 Draw a peppered moth on card. Cut it out to create a template.

life-size template

Using the template, draw forty outlines onto thin white paper. Decorate twenty as light forms and twenty as dark forms of the moth. Cut them out.

3 Put your bark rubbings on a wall to simulate a dark tree trunk and a light tree trunk.

Stick ten light forms and ten dark forms of the peppered moth on each tree trunk.

How many moths of each type can children (brought fresh to the test) pick out in one minute?

Keep a record.

Name	Number of moths picked out in 1 minute			
	dark bark		light bark	
	dark moths	light moths	dark moths	light moths
Total				

What conclusions can you draw from the test?

Each of us develops from a single cell, a fertilized egg cell. Within that one cell are the 'instructions' that help to make us both physically and to some extent mentally. The 'instructions' are held on bodies within the fertilized egg cell that are called chromosomes.

There are 46 of these chromosomes in a human cell. They are arranged in 23 pairs. One member of each pair has come from the father and the other from the mother.

These chromosomes are made of deoxyribonucleic acid, or DNA for short. Different parts of a chromosome (a DNA strand) contain the 'instructions' to control different things.

Each part is called a gene and it decides, for example, what kind of protein a cell will make or what colour our eyes will be or whether we have long or short eyelashes and so on. Just like the chromosomes they are in pairs one inherited from one parent and one from the other.

Genes do not blend to give an effect. Some genes are more forceful than others and they dominate their opposite number. Dark eyes are dominant over light eyes, for example. We thus say that the gene for light eyes is recessive.

There are a number of possible scenarios to show the combinations that might occur and these are set out in the following charts.

All dark eyes on one side of the family

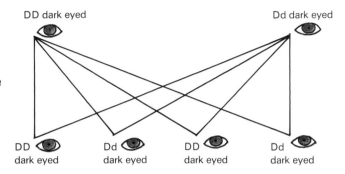

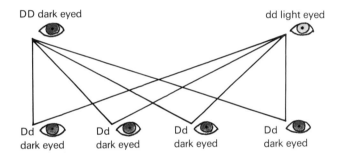

All children are dark eyed no matter what the colour of the partner's eyes.

Both parents dark eyed but with light-eyed relatives

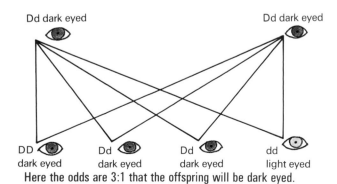

Here the odds are 3:1 that the offspring will be dark eyed.

One dark-eyed parent with light-eyed relatives, the other parent light eyed

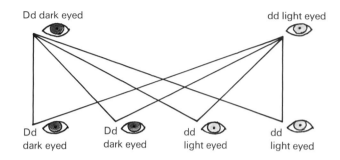

Here there is a 50:50 chance of the offspring being dark eyed.

Both parents light eyed

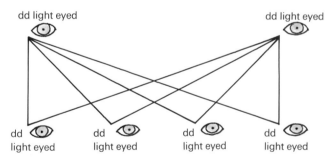

Here all the offspring will be light eyed.

Key   D = dark-eyed gene   d = light-eyed gene

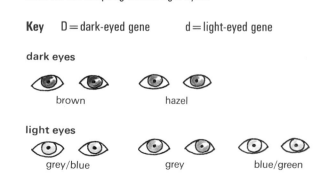

Make an eye survey

Collect statistics for child, parents and grandparents. (Sometimes children are adopted without their yet knowing and the results of the survey may need handling with discretion.)
Blue, green, grey and grey-blue eyes are light. Hazel and brown eyes are dark.

Make a table.

Grandparents		Parents		Child	
Name	eyes	Name	eyes	Name	eyes
Grandfather Smith	light	Father Smith	light	Joan Smith	dark
Grandmother Smith	light				
Grandfather Jones	light	Mother Smith	dark		
Grandmother Jones	light				

Analyse the results in relation to the charts on the previous page.

Other inherited features

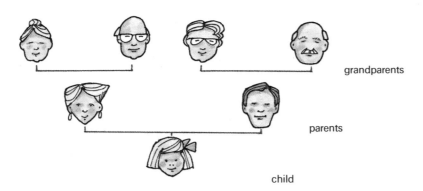

grandparents

parents

child

There are other inherited features that are relatively easy to trace.

Dominant feature	Recessive feature
dark hair	light hair / red hair
curly hair	straight hair
ability to fold tongue (see P. 57)	inability to fold tongue

Boys and girls

Of the 23 pairs of chromosomes in a cell one pair is the sex chromosomes.

In a female the two members of the pair are the same, in a male they are different. In a female they are called XX, and in a male XY.

Eggs and sperm each have half the number of chromosomes of ordinary cells — that is 23 <u>single</u> chromosomes.

Key

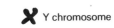 X chromosome

 Y chromosome

Mother's body cell

22 pairs

makes eggs →

22 singles   22 singles

22 + X   22 + X

22 + XX pairs

Father's body cell

22 pairs

makes sperm →

22 singles   22 singles

22 + X   22 + Y

22 + XY pairs

Fertilization

22 singles   22 singles

egg   X carrying sperm

22 pairs

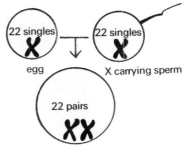

produces a female

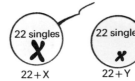

22 singles   22 singles

egg   Y carrying sperm

22 pairs

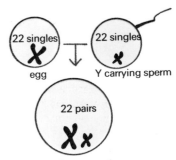

produces a male

E. J. Arnold and Son Ltd
Dewsbury Road
Leeds, LS11 5TD

Telephone: 0532 772112

Griffin and George Ltd
Bishops Meadow Road
Loughborough
Leicestershire, LE11 0RG

Telephone: 0509 233344

Philip Harris Ltd
Lynn Lane
Shenstone
Staffordshire, WS14 0EE

Telephone: 0543 480077

Berol Ltd
Oldmedow Road
Kings Lynn
Norfolk, PE30 4JR

Telephone: 0553 761221